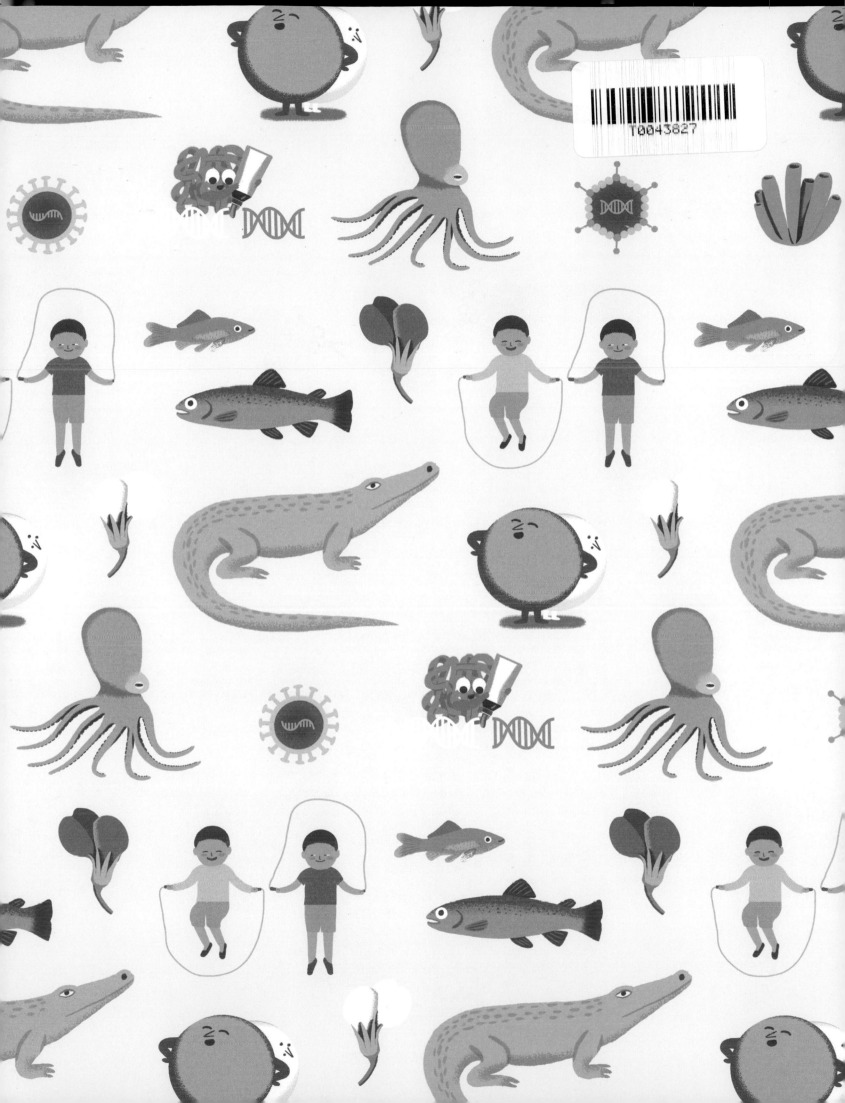

This edition published in 2024 by Flying Eye Books Ltd.
27 Westgate Street, London, E8 3RL.

First published in the German language in 2022
by von dem Knesebeck GmbH & Co. Verlag KG, a division of Média-Participations.
Original German title: *Der Code des Lebens - Alles über Gene, DNA,
Gentechnik und warum du so bist, wie du bist.*

Translated by Susan Haynes-Huber

1 3 5 7 9 10 8 6 4 2

Published by Flying Eye Books Ltd.
Printed in Poland on FSC® certified paper.

ISBN: 978-1-83874-884-5

www.flyingeyebooks.com

CARLA HÄFNER

MIEKE SCHEIER

The Code of Life

**All about genes, DNA, genetic engineering,
and why you are the way you are**

FLYING EYE BOOKS

CONTENTS

DID YOU KNOW ...

that in the beginning, you were no more than one tiny cell, invisible to the naked eye? Then that cell began to divide. One cell became two, two became four, four became eight ... And in the end, a complete organism was formed: you! But how did that first tiny cell know that it was supposed to become a human being? Why not a mouse, or an elephant, or some other, completely different creature? And if it was to become a human being, then why not one of the billions of other people on this planet? Why YOU specifically?

For a long time, scientists had no answers to these questions. But then they discovered that so-called genes exist and that it is these genes which define the characteristics of an organism. And inside the cells, they found an extraordinary substance in which all information on these genes is stored: DNA. Imagine it as a sort of blueprint for building an organism, a plan which shows what an organism is made up of, what it will look like, and what functions and features it will have. But what are genes? And what is DNA? How can DNA be small enough to fit into a single cell yet contain the details of an entire organism? How can it pass the parents' genetic information on to their children? And what happens when human beings start to change these blueprints? When they start to rewrite them? This book tells the exciting story of the discovery of DNA and explains how this discovery changed our world and us as human beings.

THE BIRTH OF GENETICS

Our story begins in 1856, in an abbey in Brünn, Austria. One of the monks who lived there was called Gregor Mendel. Mendel was anything but a typical monk: he loved mathematics, physics, and botany. As a child, he dreamed of becoming a scientist, but his parents were poor farmers and could not afford to send him to university. They expected him to take over the family farm. Entering a monastery was the best way out for Mendel. And he was lucky, because in Brünn the monks did more than just pray—they also carried out a lot of research. The abbey even sent Mendel to university for two years in Vienna. He returned to Brünn with a vast amount of knowledge about the laws of nature, mathematics, plants, and animals. And he brought something else back with him: the idea for a highly complex research project!

Soon afterwards, he began to grow pea plants of different varieties in the abbey's greenhouse: plants with violet and with white blossoms, with wrinkled and smooth-skinned peas, with yellow and with green peapods, long and short stems, and lots more. For years, he spent hours and hours every day in his greenhouse because he knew he was on his way to solving a great mystery.

Like many others in his day, Mendel longed to unlock the secrets of heredity. It was already clear that children looked like their parents and grandparents. And it was also known that plants and animals passed traits on to following generations. Farmers, for instance, used this knowledge to select the best animals for breeding. But back then, no-one could explain why this was so.

Mendel chose the pea plant for his studies as he could select plants which varied obviously in their appearance. For every trait he studied, he always had plants of two different varieties. For example, he would cross a plant with violet flowers with one with white flowers by collecting pollen from a violet blossom and brushing it onto the stigma of a white blossom. Pollen contains the male gametes (sperm cells), and these were now transferred from the stigma to the female gametes (egg cells) of the other variety to fertilize them. The new pea plants eventually grew from the fertilized egg cells. So, what do you think happened when Mendel crossed violet-flowered pea plants with white-flowered pea plants? All the new plants had violet flowers. Not a single white flower was to be seen! What had happened?

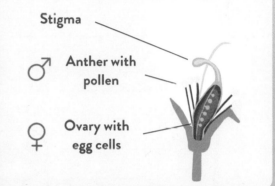

Stigma

♂ Anther with pollen

♀ Ovary with egg cells

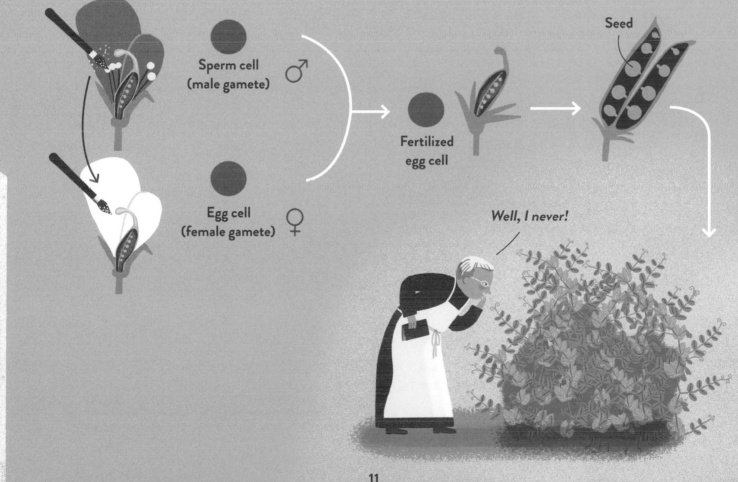

Sperm cell (male gamete) ♂

Egg cell (female gamete) ♀

Fertilized egg cell

Seed

Well, I never!

In order to find out, Mendel then crossed these newly grown plants with each other. The result was quite astonishing. The white flowers suddenly reappeared. This meant that the trait had not been lost but had somehow remained hidden. He repeated his experiment several thousand times, and it was increasingly clear that there was a recurring ratio: roughly three in four plants (that is, 75%) had violet flowers and one in four plants (that is, 25%) had white ones. A ratio of 3 to 1!

Mendel examined a total of seven different traits in his pea plants, and again and again he saw the same results: in the second generation, the pea plants all looked identical, like one of the parent plants, and in the following generation, both variants appeared— always in a ratio of 3 to 1.

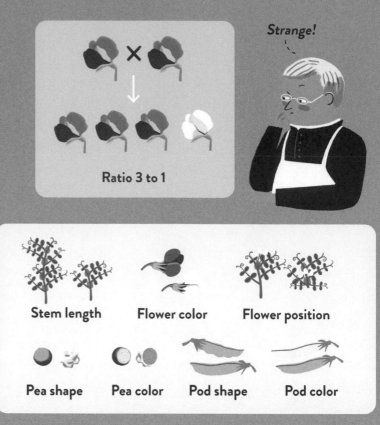

Strange!

Ratio 3 to 1

Stem length	Flower color	Flower position

Pea shape	Pea color	Pod shape	Pod color

FATHER PLANT   MOTHER PLANT

GAMETES FUSE

NEW PEA PLANT

Mendel thought deeply about this. Obviously, something in the gametes contained information on the traits and passed it on to the next generation when the plants were crossed. Tiny particles of some kind. He named them **elements**.

And Mendel realized something else. Since he had achieved the same result for all traits, the numbers had to follow a uniform rule! Then he found a possible explanation for the recurring ratio: there had to be two of these elements for each trait. A pair! But the parents only passed on one element to their offspring, and it was pure coincidence which of the two was handed down. In other words, the young pea plants inherited one element from the father plant and one from the mother, and therefore had two elements, like their parents.

But the elements existed in two variants: in the case of flower color, for example, 'violet' and 'white.' If a plant receives two elements of the same kind from its parents, the situation is clear: two violet elements will produce violet blossoms, two white elements will result in white blossoms.

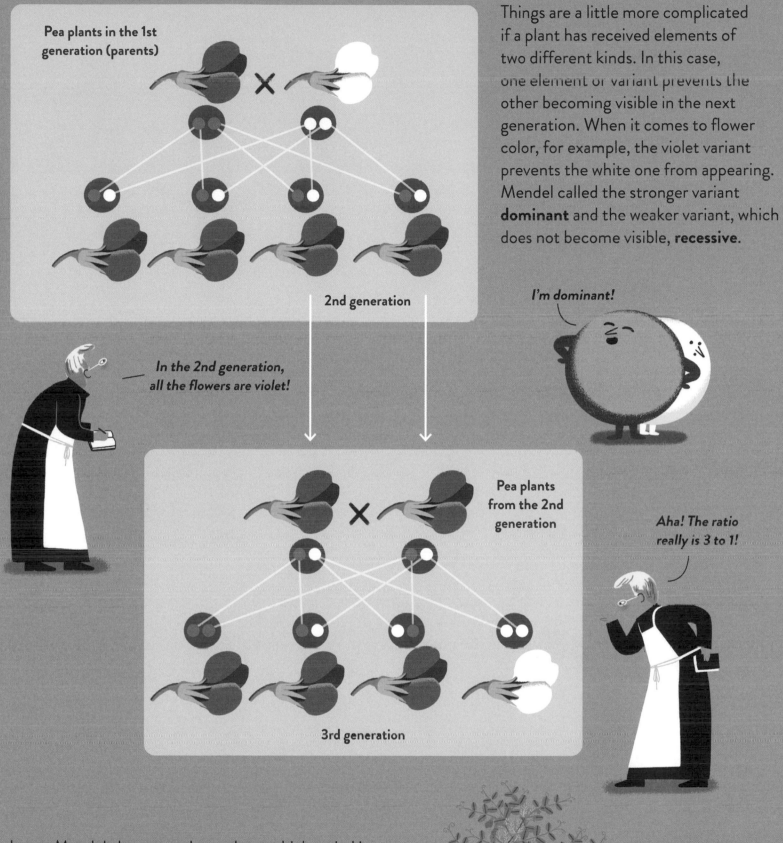

Pea plants in the 1st generation (parents)

2nd generation

In the 2nd generation, all the flowers are violet!

Pea plants from the 2nd generation

3rd generation

I'm dominant!

Aha! The ratio really is 3 to 1!

Things are a little more complicated if a plant has received elements of two different kinds. In this case, one element or variant prevents the other becoming visible in the next generation. When it comes to flower color, for example, the violet variant prevents the white one from appearing. Mendel called the stronger variant **dominant** and the weaker variant, which does not become visible, **recessive**.

Later, Mendel also crossed pea plants which varied in two or three traits. Based on the mathematical ratios, he was able to show that the different traits were inherited independently of each other. In the case of flower color, for example, it makes no difference whether the plant has a short or a long stem and whether the peas are wrinkly or smooth. The expression of one trait has no influence on the expression of the other traits.

Mendel published his findings, but no-one paid much attention to his work. The results of his experiments were not rediscovered until 40 years later, long after Mendel's death, and only then did people realize the great significance of his observations. Although Mendel had no idea what the so-called elements were made of or where exactly they were located, he was the first to discover that they existed. And it was these elements which determined what the pea plants looked like and which were passed down from the parent plants to their offspring according to fixed rules. Later, Mendel's elements were renamed **genes**. Mendel really had discovered the fundamental principles of genetics. And this was not some unusual phenomenon that only happened in pea plants: genes are the carriers of genetic information for all other organisms, too. They contain information on the characteristics of the organism. And the laws of heredity explain how these genes are passed on from one generation to the next—and it's the same for humans as it is for pea plants.

You, too, inherited genes from your parents—one half from your father and the other half from your mother. These genes define what you look like and make you the person you are. So, now you know why children often look like their parents or grandparents, and why siblings are alike: it's all because of the genes! What Mendel found out about heredity marked the birth of a new science— genetics. This is why today Mendel is sometimes called the **father of genetics**!

We all have genes!

The elements Mendel discovered (later renamed genes) are responsible for passing on traits from one generation to the next. There are two copies of each gene, one inherited from the father and the other from the mother. Mendel's laws of inheritance describe how the genes are passed on.

The gene copy which suppresses the effect of the other copy is called **dominant**.

The gene copy which is suppressed is called **recessive**.

A LOOK THROUGH THE MICROSCOPE

To find genes, we have to look inside the cells. Cells are the building blocks of life. Your body is made up of cells, too, billions and billions of tiny cells. Your skin, your muscles, your bones, your brain—they all consist of cells. In the 18th century, people invented better and better microscopes, and as a result, it was possible to find out a lot more about our cells. Scientists discovered that every cell contained a round structure. They named it the **nucleus**. Inside the nucleus, they saw one or more smaller rounded bodies, which they called **nucleoli**. In addition, they discovered that the nucleus of the cell was surrounded by a liquid, called the cell plasma.

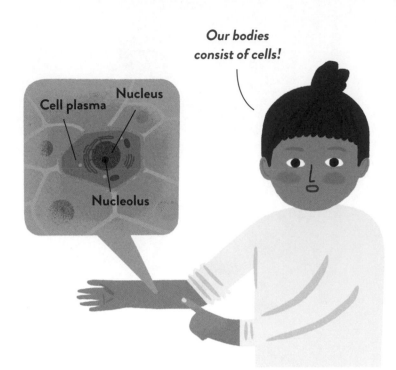

Our bodies consist of cells!

Cell plasma • Nucleus • Nucleolus

Walther Flemming, a biologist working in Kiel, in northern Germany, was a prominent researcher at that time. He spent many hours examining cells under a microscope. One day, while experimenting with a new process for staining the cells with dye so that he could see them more clearly, he discovered something strange within the cell nucleus. It absorbed the dye and turned an intense blue. Flemming called it **chromatin**, which is derived from the Greek word *chroma* and simply means 'color.'

Flemming examined the chromatin in various cells and observed what happened to it when cells divided. Cell division is important because it is the only way for bodies to grow. One cell becomes two, two cells become four, and so on.

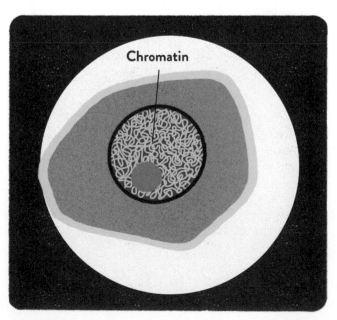

Chromatin

Flemming observed this process of cell division under a microscope and made an exciting discovery:

1

Shortly before the cell divided, the envelope enclosing the nucleus suddenly disintegrated, and the appearance of the blue-stained chromatin changed. Instead of forming a fine, thread-like network, the threads were now bundled together.

2

The threads grew thicker, and soon individual structures, each made up of two threads, could be seen. These structures are called **chromosomes**.

Parent cell

3

Then the chromosomes moved and formed a straight line in the center of the cell, as though they were preparing to dance.

4

At the same time, thin threads were extended from the ends of the cells (the so-called 'poles'). These threads grabbed the chromosomes from both sides, pulled them apart, and drew the individual threads to the opposite poles.

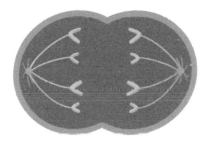

5

Each chromosome now consisted of only one thread, and a new envelope began to form around the chromosomes at each pole.

Two daughter cells

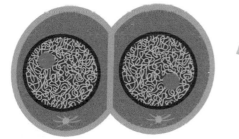

6

The chromosomes returned to their original form, and the envelope became more and more pinched together in the middle until finally it split into two.

The end result was that one cell had become two: two so-called daughter cells. Flemming named this process **mitosis**. Later, it became clear why the chromosomes consisted of two threads at the beginning but only had one thread after the cell had divided: undetected by the microscope, the threads had duplicated themselves before the cell split. And this duplication of the chromosomes is important! It ensures that although the cell divides, each daughter cell has the same number of chromosomes as the parent cell.

Scientist Theodor Boveri, who carried out his research in the German city of Würzburg around 1900, was interested in another process: the formation of gametes. This process is called **meiosis**. We came across the gametes when we were describing Mendel's experiments. These are very special cells because they can generate a new life. Observing them under the microscope, Boveri realized something very important: the number of chromosomes was halved when the gametes were formed. The chromosomes were only present in double the quantity again following the fusion of the male and female gametes.

MEIOSIS: The number of chromosomes is halved during formation of the gametes

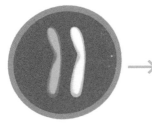

Double set of chromosomes

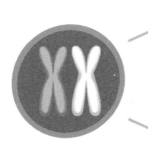

Doubling of the threads

Chromosomes are separated

Gametes (single set of chromosomes)

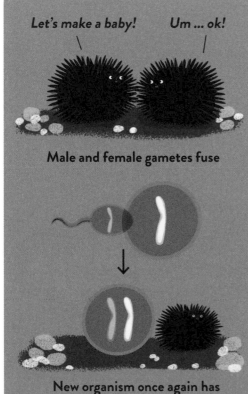

Let's make a baby!   Um ... ok!

Male and female gametes fuse

New organism once again has a double set of chromosomes

In other words, every cell of an organism always contains the same number of chromosomes. But gametes only have half as many chromosomes as other cells, and the double number of chromosomes is only present again after fusion of the gametes. But just a minute ... haven't we seen this before? Yes, remember Mendel and his pea plants! Only then, we called them elements instead of chromosomes. Theodor Boveri and his American colleague Walter Sutton also realized this connection. Together, in 1904, they put forward the theory that these elements (later named genes) must be in the chromosomes.

The elements must be in the chromosomes!

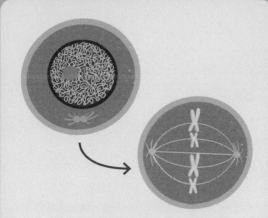

Chromosomes are only
visible during cell division and arise
through concentration of chromatin

Scientists later discovered that humans have a total of 46 chromosomes, which come in 23 pairs (that is, each chromosome in duplicate). In each of these 23 pairs, one chromosome comes from the father and the other from the mother, and chromosome pair 23 plays a special role, because these are the sex chromosomes. In humans, there are two types: the X chromosome and the somewhat shorter Y chromosome. The combination determines the chromosomal sex or gender: boys usually have one X and one Y chromosome, and girls have two X chromosomes. However, there are exceptions and sometimes an individual identifies with a gender different to that defined by the chromosomes.

A diagram or photo of the chromosomes of a cell is called a karyogram.

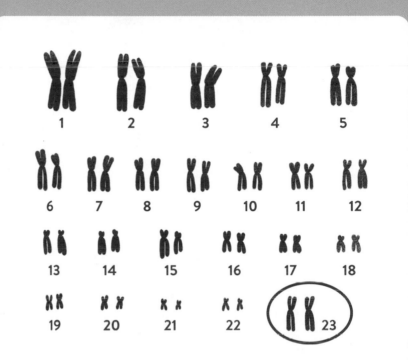

Sex chromosomes:

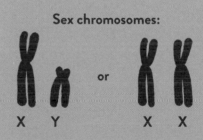

X   Y   or   X   X

Each human body cell has 23 chromosome pairs, in other words, a total of 46 chromosomes. The gametes only have half that number (23 chromosomes).

Mitosis is the process by which body cells divide. Mitosis occurs when an organism grows or cells are renewed.

Meiosis is the process by which male and female gametes are formed. The gametes can generate a new life.

IN THE FLY ROOM

Scientists now understood that genes must be in chromosomes. But how could we find them? And what exactly were these genes? Biologist Thomas Morgan was extremely sceptical. He set out to examine Mendel's findings using fruit flies and, in 1908, he began his own research in a laboratory at Columbia University in New York.

Just like Mendel with his peas, Morgan first needed to understand what differed from one fly to another, and how this passed on to further generations. So he began to breed flies, and soon the laboratory benches were full of little bottles with flies in them. More and more every day! Soon, everyone was calling it the Fly Room.

Among these hundreds and hundreds of insects, the scientist discovered individual flies that looked different from the others. Random changes to the genes of these flies had occurred. Morgan would find flies with all kinds of unusual features, including shorter wings, crooked legs, or missing eyes. These special flies were perfect for Morgan's research into heredity because the distinctive features made it easy to distinguish their offspring from the original form.

In his experiments, Morgan saw the same ratios as Mendel ... but he discovered something more! Morgan crossed a male fly with white eyes and a female with red eyes, and then crossed their offspring with each other. He found that white eyes were only ever found in males. He repeated the experiment. Not a single female with white eyes! Obviously, white eye color was linked to the gender of the fly. And gender depends on the sex chromosomes (X and Y). This meant that the genetic change had to have occurred on one of the sex chromosomes. Based on the precise figures from his experiments, he concluded that it had to be the X chromosome. Morgan had succeeded in assigning a gene to a chromosome! And that was just the beginning. He observed that the traits he was examining were not always passed on independent of each other, but in groups. For example, short wings and black body color were inherited together. Altogether, Morgan was able to divide the heredity of the different traits into four groups.

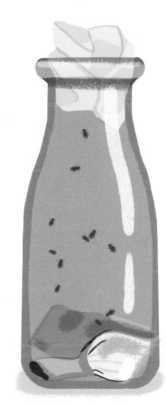

And guess how many pairs of chromosomes a fruit fly has: four! Was this a coincidence? Morgan didn't think so! He was convinced that the reason why traits were passed on together was that the genes responsible for them were located on the same chromosomes. He imagined the genes strung on the chromosomes like pearls on a necklace.

But Morgan and his colleagues were not only able to find out which genes lay together on the same chromosome; they also identified which genes were located close to each other on the chromosomes and which were further apart. They were able to assign the genes to specific locations on the chromosomes and compiled the first so-called gene maps.

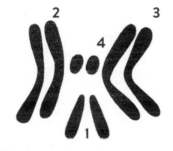

Chromosomes of the fruit fly

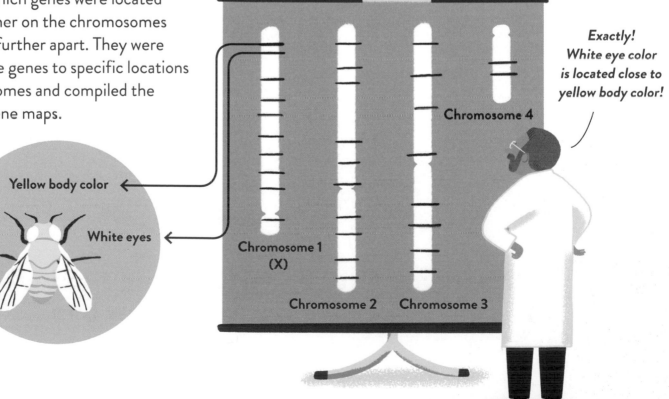

Exactly! White eye color is located close to yellow body color!

Yellow body color

White eyes

Chromosome 1 (X)

Chromosome 2

Chromosome 3

Chromosome 4

WHAT GENES ARE MADE OF

It was now clear that Mendel's elements really did exist. The genes were part of the chromosomes. But what were they made of? In the year 1869, a doctor called Friedrich Miescher made an exciting discovery in Tübingen while conducting experiments on white blood cells extracted from pus on fresh wound dressings.

People already knew that protein was a major component of cells, but with the aid of his experiments, he hoped to learn more about proteins and their function in the cells. Instead of proteins, he found something else in his test tubes: a mysterious white deposit. This deposit originated from the cell nuclei and did not behave at all like a protein. Initially, Miescher named it nuclein, but it was later renamed **nucleic acid**. Nucleic acid could be frozen and thawed again, but it decomposed rapidly at room temperature. Miescher was lucky that it was winter at the time and icy cold in his laboratory. Otherwise, the nucleic acid would have decomposed too quickly for him to have discovered its existence.

Miescher soon found a new source of nucleic acid for his research: salmon sperm! It contained huge numbers of male sperm cells, from which Miescher was able to extract large quantities of nucleic acid. It was hard work, though. Without the invention of refrigerators, Miescher could only carry out his experiments in the winter months. He'd get up in the middle of the night and, armed with nets, go fishing for salmon along a river. Then he'd return to his laboratory, throw open the windows, and carry out his experiments in the bitter cold. Miescher had discovered nucleic acid! But what was its purpose in the cell?

Almost 75 years passed before it was possible to answer this question. In 1944, the mystery was finally solved: in an experiment, Oswald Avery demonstrated that nucleic acid, or more precisely **deoxyribonucleic acid (DNA)**, was the substance that genes were made of, which defines what we look like and which is passed on from parents to their children. This was the substance scientists had been searching for so many years! And they learned more about DNA—namely what it consists of: sugar (deoxyribose), phosphate residues, and so-called bases (adenine, thymine, cytosine, guanine). We're in the field of chemistry here ... but don't worry! Simply imagine these elements as pieces of a jigsaw puzzle you can move around. And the names are just names for these individual jigsaw pieces.

By the way, in addition to DNA, scientists also found a second type of nucleic acid: **RNA (ribonucleic acid)**. RNA also plays an important role in our story, but more about that a little later. The box at the bottom of this page shows the difference between DNA and RNA: the sugar in DNA is deoxyribose, which is why it is called deoxyribonucleic acid. RNA, on the other hand, contains the sugar ribose. Hence the name ribonucleic acid! And there is another difference: the base thymine does not occur in RNA. Instead, RNA contains the base uracil.

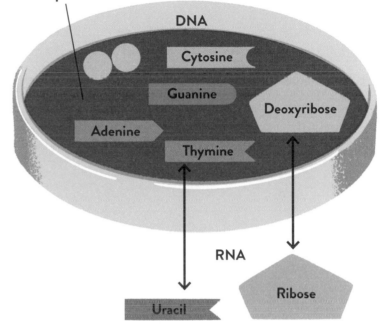

The DNA in the cell nucleus is the main element of the chromosomes. It is the carrier of the genetic information. DNA consists of the sugar deoxyribose, phosphate residues, and four bases (adenine, thymine, cytosine, and guanine).

There are two sorts of nucleic acid: DNA (deoxyribonucleic acid) and RNA (ribonucleic acid).

The structure of RNA is a bit different from that of DNA. RNA contains ribose instead of the sugar deoxyribose. And it contains the base uracil instead of thymine.

IN THE LAB: SOLVING THE DNA PUZZLE

But how was it possible for DNA to contain all of the genetic information of a living organism? In those days, many scientists were eager to solve this puzzle because it was the key to an even greater mystery: life itself.

Researchers Rosalind Franklin and Maurice Wilkins were working in a laboratory in London, where they examined the structure of DNA using x-rays. They took DNA in solid, crystalline form and x-rayed it to produce diffraction images, hoping to learn more about its structure and form. You can imagine these images as like the shadows you can produce on a wall in a dark room by shining a torch on an object or on your hands.

One day, Wilkins was delivering a lecture on his research work and showed a diffraction image of DNA. In the audience was a man called James Watson. The image made such a strong impression on him that he couldn't get it out of his mind. Although the quality of the image was very poor, it revealed the regular structure of DNA. A short time later, Watson seized the chance to work in a laboratory in Cambridge so that he could conduct his own research into the structure of DNA. He was determined that he would be the first to discover what DNA looked like. At the laboratory, Watson met researcher Francis Crick. The two men talked endlessly about what DNA might be made up of and were obsessed with solving this mystery. Soon, they were given a separate room in the laboratory for their experiments. Here, they spent hours building models using simple components like metal plates, pieces of wood, small balls, wire, and screws.

At the same time, in his laboratory at Columbia University, New York, Erwin Chargaff was investigating the structure of DNA in various organisms. He found that it always contained the same elements: sugar, phosphate residues, and the four bases (adenine, thymine, cytosine, and guanine). And he discovered another interesting fact: two of the four bases were always found in the same quantity. The amount of adenine was always the same as that of thymine, and the amount of guanine the same as that of cytosine. How remarkable!

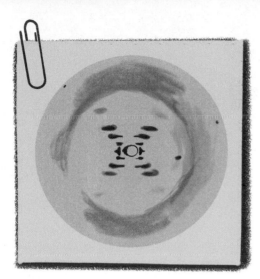

Photo 51

But let's return to Watson and Crick: one day, Watson visited Wilkins in his laboratory to discuss the structure of DNA and Wilkins showed him one of Franklin's images, the famous Photo 51. When Watson saw it, it was immediately clear to him that the shape of DNA had to be a helix: a strand twisted into a spiral, like the thread of a screw. Shortly after, Watson declared that DNA must be a double helix consisting of two strands. As genes and chromosomes occur in pairs and cells duplicate, a model consisting of two strands made more sense.

Watson and Crick now set out to develop a model of DNA. Once again, they considered how the individual components might be connected. The strands were formed of sugar and phosphate residues, but how did the four bases fit into the model? Were the strands on the inside and the bases on the outside? Or was it the other way around? And how were the bases bonded together? Then Watson noticed that a pair comprising adenine and thymine had the same form as a pair comprising guanine and cytosine, which told them that two bases always belonged together as a pair. And suddenly, everything made sense: the strands were outside, the bases on the inside, located opposite each other. Adenine formed a pair with thymine and guanine with cytosine. Always the same two partners. Do you remember Chargaff's discovery that these two bases were always present in the same quantity? That made sense, too. Everything fitted together perfectly!

By March 1953, Watson and Crick had solved the mystery of the structure of DNA. The DNA double helix looked like a long, twisted rope ladder. The strands made from sugar and phosphate residues formed the two ropes on the right and left, while the pairs of bases were the rungs of the ladder.

In other words, the blueprint or recipe for all living organisms is a simple sequence of bases, a secret code made up of four letters: A(denine), T(hymine), G(uanine) and C(ytosine)! And the nucleus of every single cell contains a copy of this blueprint.

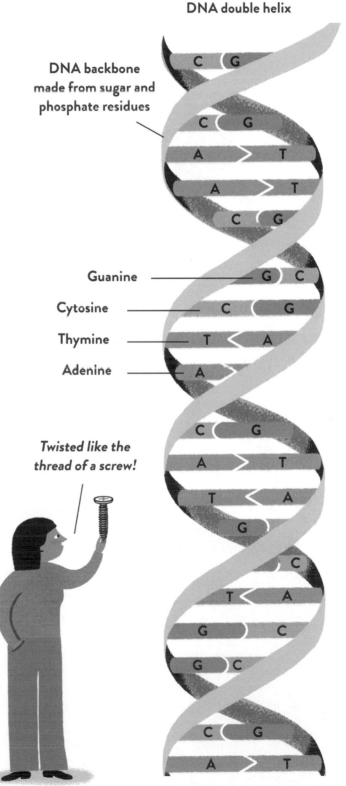

DNA double helix

DNA backbone made from sugar and phosphate residues

Guanine

Cytosine

Thymine

Adenine

Twisted like the thread of a screw!

THE ZIP FUNCTION

But Watson and Crick were already thinking one step ahead. The arrangement of the bases in pairs in DNA really was a striking feature—and it fascinated them. The sequence of bases on one strand of DNA also revealed the sequence of the bases on the opposite strand. This arrangement in pairs was the key to understanding how DNA could be duplicated and passed on to the next generation when cells divided. And that is important, because if an organism is to grow and one cell is to become a multitude of cells, every single cell must contain the same genetic information.

Imagine DNA as a zip. The bases in the DNA are like the teeth of the zip. To duplicate the DNA, the zip opens and a new strand with the opposite bases is formed for each original strand. Matching bases are added to the new strand. And hey presto! Soon, there are no longer two, but four strands. One DNA double helix has become two. In this way, after cell division, the identical DNA is present in each of the two cells. This whole process is called **replication**.

A perfect fit!

DNA strand opens

Bases are added

Two DNA strands are formed

Replication is the duplication of the DNA before cell division and ensures that, following cell division, the DNA present in each of the two daughter cells is identical.

26

CRACKING THE GENETIC CODE

We have seen that there is a secret code hidden in DNA. This code is made up of four different letters (bases) and defines, for example, whether our hair is straight or curly and whether we have blue or brown eyes. And it is this code that specifies that we have hair and eyes in the first place. But how? Does the code read something like 'Eyes green' (written in DNA letter code, of course) and then, as if by magic, we get green eyes? How is a code made up of letters translated into a physical feature?

Scientists George Beadle and Edward Tatum investigated this in their laboratory at Stanford University in California. And in 1941, they had the answer. They found out that the code defined which proteins were produced inside a cell.

Proteins play a very important role in our bodies. To ensure that our bodies work as intended, hundreds and hundreds of chemical reactions need to take place in the individual cells. You could say that our bodies are like chemical factories. Proteins are the substances which allow the chemical reactions to take place in the factory (as so-called enzymes): these substances attach themselves to the enzymes and are then converted into new substances. But proteins also perform many other tasks. The protein collagen, for example, is found in tendons, ligaments, cartilage, and bone and can strengthen the cells. Haemoglobin, the substance that colors our blood red, is a protein which transports oxygen in the red blood corpuscles, ensuring that every cell in the body is supplied with oxygen. Antibodies are proteins, too. They are important in the fight against enemy germs. And when proteins bond with dyes, for example, they can determine eye or hair color. Proteins can also be biological messengers, allowing cells to communicate with each other.

Just imagine: an organism is made up of billions of tiny cells which all have their own tasks and functions. What would happen if the cells could not coordinate their actions?

Why are my eyes green?

Proteins are responsible!

And who decides what proteins are produced?

The genes! Thanks to specific sections of DNA.

Proteins consist of long chains of tiny building blocks called **amino acids**. A total of 20 different amino acids are used in varying combinations. The chains are also twisted multiple times, folded together, and look very complicated!

By the way, proteins are manufactured in little 'protein factories' in the cells, called **ribosomes**. These factories are located in the cell plasma (the liquid surrounding the nucleus of the cell).

So, if the proteins are manufactured in the cell plasma, how does the information from the DNA get from the cell nucleus to the plasma? In other words, how do the ribosomes know which proteins to make?

In 1960, François Jacob and Sydney Brenner, researchers in Cambridge, discovered that RNA, which is very similar to DNA, acts as a messenger. For this reason, it is also known as **messenger RNA**. When a certain protein is to be produced, a copy of the DNA segment containing the information for this protein is made. This copy is the messenger RNA! And the copying process is called **transcription**.

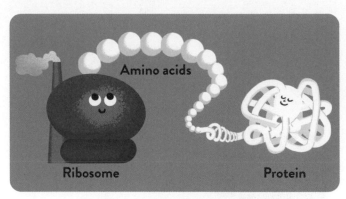

Amino acids
Ribosome
Protein

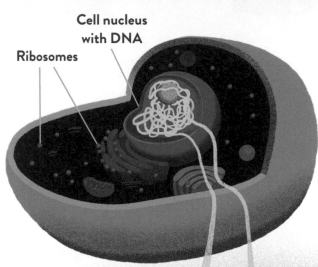

Cell nucleus with DNA
Ribosomes

What do you want me to build?

The messenger RNA will bring you the blueprint!

Messenger RNA →

I got the info!

Once the messenger RNA has been formed, it wanders from the cell nucleus, through the membrane of the nucleus, into the cell plasma, and right to the little protein factories, the ribosomes.

In the ribosomes, the information from the messenger RNA needs to be translated into a protein. But how? The obvious conclusion, of course, is that the sequence of letters plays a key role. It defines the sequence of the amino acids and thus also which protein is produced. However, there is not one letter for each amino acid. If there were, there would have to be 20 letters (bases), one for each amino acid. But there are only four! The scientists discovered that in each case, a group of three letters contained the information on an amino acid. And soon they succeeded in assigning three-letter codes to all amino acids. The code was cracked!

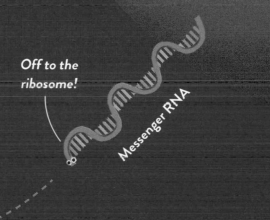

Off to the ribosome!

Messenger RNA

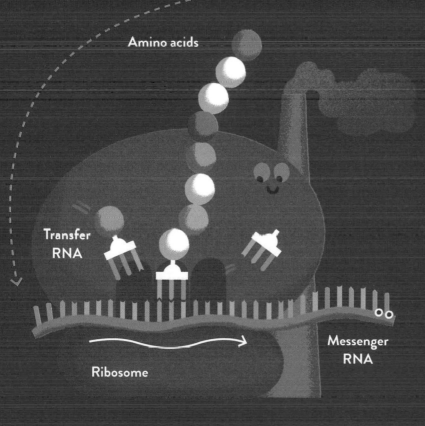

Amino acids

Transfer RNA

Ribosome

Messenger RNA

In the protein factories, the proteins are manufactured with the help of this code from the messenger RNA. For every combination of three letters, the factories contain a matching adapter (called **transfer RNA**) which docks onto the messenger RNA on one side and provides the matching amino acid on the other. In other words, as the messenger RNA is read from beginning to end, the chain of amino acids which make up the protein grows.

This entire production process is called **translation**. You probably know the word 'translation' used to describe the process of taking a word or text in one language and converting it into another. Well, here, a three-letter code is converted into the name of an amino acid.

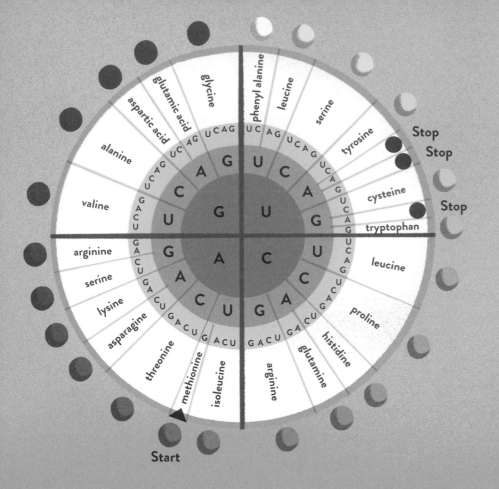

Start

With the help of this code table, you can translate the letter code on the messenger RNA yourself. In each case, three letters stand for one amino acid. Try cracking the code GCA. Start in the middle and find the letter G. Move one ring outwards to locate C, and then again for A. Found it? The code GCA stands for the amino acid alanine! In the protein production process, this means that when the letter code GCA is located on the messenger RNA, the amino acid alanine is formed at the ribosomes.

Can you crack these codes, too? GUC, AGC, AUG, UAG. See page 68 for the answers.

So, what had our researchers discovered? They had found out that the arrangement of the four letters on the DNA specifies which proteins are produced within the body, and that it is these proteins which determine our traits. In other words, we can imagine DNA as a blueprint showing the structure of an organism and how it functions. The arrangement of the four letters for the bases is the language in which the diagram is written. And this language is the same for all living organisms, which is why it is also referred to as the Code of Life.

Amino acids are the building blocks of the proteins. Proteins perform a wide range of tasks within the cell. They consist of long amino acid chains. The process of producing proteins at the ribosomes is called translation.

When a protein is being formed, a copy is made of the DNA segment which contains the information for this protein (transcription).

This copy wanders from the cell nucleus to the ribosomes, where the protein is made based on the three-letter code (translation).

The genetic code is the information on the proteins encoded as a sequence of letters on the DNA. In each case, three letters (bases) provide the information on one amino acid. The genetic code is the same for all organisms.

PACKED AWAY IN THE NUCLEUS

If you unrolled all 46 human chromosomes and placed them end to end as one DNA thread, it would be almost two meters long. In our cells, however, the DNA is pressed tightly together in the cell nucleus, which has a diameter of only about one hundredth of a millimeter. How is that possible? Just think how many meters of yarn there are in one small ball of wool. The DNA is packed into the cell in a similar way.

DNA does not float around freely in the nucleus. Instead, it is coiled up on ball-shaped proteins like wool on a reel. These proteins are called **histones**. They make sure that the long DNA threads don't become tangled up and that everything is kept neatly inside the nucleus. At the same time, they control which segments of the DNA can be copied to RNA.

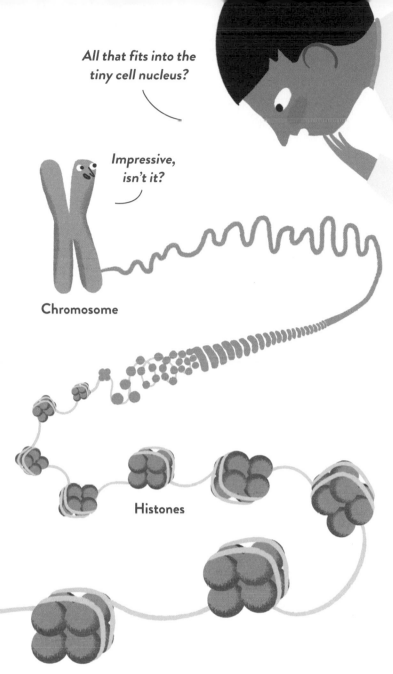

All that fits into the tiny cell nucleus?

Impressive, isn't it?

Chromosome

Histones

DNA double helix

DNA strand with base pairs

Thymine

Adenine

Guanine

Cytosine

Histones are proteins in the cell nucleus onto which the DNA is coiled.

31

MISTAKES HAPPEN

Have you ever made a mistake? It's very likely you have because everyone makes mistakes now and then. The protein which copies the DNA when a cell divides (the DNA polymerase) sometimes makes the mistake of accidentally inserting a wrong base. This happens about once every 100 million bases. Usually, these mistakes are detected by special repair proteins. Then the incorrect base is removed and replaced with the right one. Sometimes, however, the repair proteins don't detect the mistake, and the incorrect base remains in the DNA of a cell. This random change in the bases is called a **mutation**.

Although some mutations have no effect whatsoever, others can lead to illness. Cancer is one example of a very serious disease which can be caused by mutations in the DNA. Sooner or later, as the result of an accumulation of various mutations in the DNA, the cell functions are disrupted and the cell begins to multiply in an uncontrolled manner. Tumors grow and spread throughout the body, which can sadly sometimes be fatal.

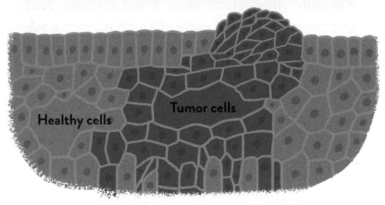

A tumor arises because of uncontrolled cell growth

Environmental influences can encourage the development of cancer. For example, sunlight is pleasant but the UV radiation in sunlight is dangerous. It can damage the DNA in the cells of your skin, trigger mutations, and, in the worst case, cause skin cancer. That is why it is very important to apply sunscreen to protect your skin against UV radiation.

Mutations in the body's cells only have an influence on the organism in which these mutations take place. But if these mutations occur in the gametes, parents pass them on to their children. And in turn, the children can pass them on to their children. In this way, some mutations become the cause of hereditary diseases.

Sickle cell disease is an example of how changing just one letter in the DNA leads to a very serious hereditary illness. The mistake that occurs in sickle cell disease is that the base A (adenine) is replaced with T (thymine) in the gene responsible for the production of haemoglobin, the protein which colors our blood red. Red blood corpuscles flow through all your blood vessels, and the haemoglobin in the red blood corpuscles is responsible for the transportation of oxygen. It is essential because every cell in your body needs oxygen in order to survive. In sickle cell disease, the base sequence GAG is mutated to GTG. As a result, the amino acid valine is produced instead of glutamic acid.

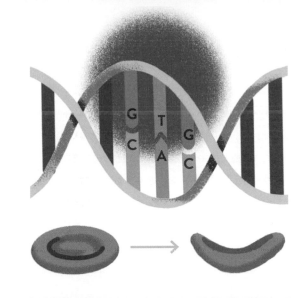

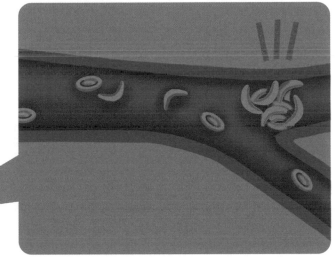

This means that the haemoglobin does not fold normally. Instead of being round, the red blood cells look like a sickle (a C-shaped farm tool). These sickle-shaped red blood cells don't live as long as round ones. They are also less flexible, which means they can't pass through narrow blood vessels as easily and sometimes get stuck. This leads to tiny clots. The organs are not adequately supplied with blood, and people with the disease suffer extreme pain and their organs are damaged due to the lack of oxygen. Sadly, people with this disease often die very young.

A mutation is a change in the base sequence on the DNA. It can occur spontaneously (which means without an external cause) or can be triggered by the effects of chemicals or high-energy radiation (radioactivity, UV radiation).

Mutations in the gametes are passed on to the following generations. They can be the cause of hereditary diseases.

ABOUT DIVERSITY

We have read a lot about the problems mutations can cause, but mutations are not always bad. They are a precondition for the diversity of life here on our planet Earth. Without mutations, human beings wouldn't even exist! And all this has to do with **evolution** ... but what exactly is evolution? To understand this, let's take another trip back in time, to meet a scientist called Charles Darwin.

Darwin spent the years from 1831 to 1836 on a voyage of discovery, predominantly around South America, on board the expedition ship *Beagle*. He studied the plants and animals in the areas the ship visited and, based on his observations, he put forward a theory of how life might have developed on Earth. In 1859, he published his famous book about this theory, called *On the Origin of Species*. Darwin believed that all living beings were descended from one common ancestor. According to him, they constantly developed, because occasionally variants of traits occurred. And sometimes, these variants offered an advantage when it came to survival. If there was a drought, then the animals that needed less water had an advantage. They survived and passed their genes on to their offspring. If there was flooding, the creatures that could swim best had an advantage—and so on. In other words, when environmental conditions changed, variants best suited to the new conditions survived while less suited variants were lost. There was a process of **natural selection** which favored variants that were better at adapting to the new environment. This was how living beings developed over the generations. Darwin visualized this as a kind of Tree of Life which branched out as species developed over time.

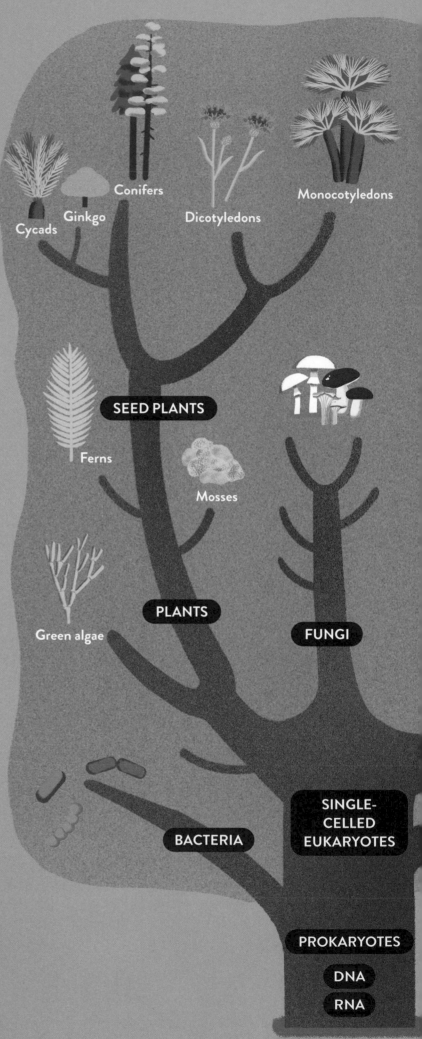

Cycads

Ginkgo

Conifers

Dicotyledons

Monocotyledons

SEED PLANTS

Ferns

Mosses

Green algae

PLANTS

FUNGI

BACTERIA

SINGLE-CELLED EUKARYOTES

PROKARYOTES

DNA

RNA

34

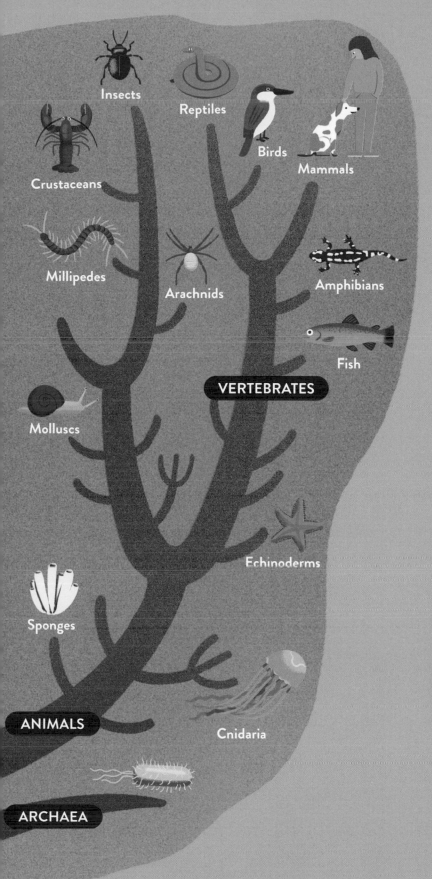

Insects

Reptiles

Birds

Mammals

Crustaceans

Millipedes

Arachnids

Amphibians

Fish

VERTEBRATES

Molluscs

Echinoderms

Sponges

ANIMALS

Cnidaria

ARCHAEA

Evolution refers to the origin of species through random changes to DNA (mutation) and natural selection.

Later, it became clear that variants of traits are caused by mutations. Mutations ensure genetic diversity, and genetic diversity allows organisms to adapt to changing environmental conditions. A lack of diversity, on the other hand, threatens the survival of species because the ability to adapt is lost. This applies to all living beings: it is a fundamental principle of nature.

Let's return to the subject of sickle cell disease, a prime example of evolution in human beings. We know that sickle cell disease is a very serious illness, but this only applies to people who have the mutation on both the paternal and the maternal chromosome. In other words, people who have inherited two copies of the faulty gene. People who only have the mutation on one of their chromosomes usually have no symptoms at all. In fact, the mutation even has a positive side-effect in this case, because it provides protection against another serious disease: malaria. Malaria is caused by tiny germs called plasmodia, which are transmitted by the Anopheles mosquito. Every year, millions of people die of this disease.

Distribution of malaria

Distribution of sickle cell disease

In areas where the Anopheles mosquito is particularly common, including parts of Africa, people with this mutation have a major survival advantage. Over time, the mutation has spread so strongly in these regions that most of the inhabitants now carry the mutation. On the other hand, in regions where the Anopheles mosquito is not found and where, as a result, malaria does not normally occur, the mutation is extremely rare as it offers no advantage.

PRISONERS OF OUR GENES?

We have already seen that what we look like is already firmly anchored in our DNA. But what about our behaviour or our personality or how long we live for? Is all that determined in advance, too, or do these things depend on our environment and our lifestyle? The fundamental question is: is our future already laid down in the genetic blueprint or does it lie in our own hands?

In the year 1979, a behavioural psychologist called Thomas Bouchard came across an interesting article in his local newspaper. It told the story of identical twins who were separated immediately after birth and only reunited some 30 years later. The case was impressive because it turned out that there were many bizarre similarities in the lives of these men. They had both married women called Linda. One had a son named James Alan, while the son of the other twin was called James Allan. Each twin had a dog and had named it Toy. They were both chain smokers and preferred the same brand of cigarettes, and they both hated baseball. Both enjoyed woodwork and had built similar benches around a tree in their gardens. Simply a weird series of coincidences? Or did this reveal the secret power of genes?

Bouchard launched a study, for which he needed identical twins exactly like those in the article he had read: twins who were separated at birth and only reunited years later. These twins were ideal for a study on the influence of genetics because they had the same genes but had grown up in different environments. This meant that if physical and psychological tests showed that there were similarities between them, these could not be attributed to the influence of their environment. Instead, they must have their origin in their DNA. Bouchard compared his findings with the results of tests on identical twins who had not been separated at birth and therefore had been subject to the same environmental influences.

Amazing!

Bouchard and his team examined more than 100 sets of twins, and the results were astounding: the separated twins achieved similar results in intelligence tests, personality tests, their preferences, their behaviour, personal, attitudes and temperament. Often, the researchers noted that the twins shared small but unique characteristics: the same distinctive giggle, the same unusually deep voice, the same weird sense of humour, the same way of sitting down or moving, the same taste in music and books, the same extravagant way of dressing. It was both fascinating and a little strange. Obviously, the genes did have a considerable influence on these characteristics. Altogether, Bouchard and his team discovered that around half of personality and behavioral traits were determined by genes, the other half by the environment. When it came to intelligence, there was an even better match between twins, meaning that the influence of the genes is probably higher.

The researchers set out to identify which genes are responsible for our personality and our behaviour. For example, in people who were curious and adventurous, they found a link with a specific gene variant, which became known as the Wanderlust or risk-taking gene. However, this gene variant is not found in everyone who has these characteristics, and it can also be found in people who are not particularly curious or adventurous.

The fact is that there is not one gene for curiosity and one gene for anxiety: no single gene can ever be responsible for such complex characteristics. The influence of the environment also plays a role in the development of a personality trait. The same applies to many illnesses—including high blood pressure, diabetes, and cancer—where many different genes combined with environmental influences determine whether the disease eventually breaks out.

Personality and behavior are determined approximately 50% by our genes and 50% by the environment.

Complex characteristics are the result of many different genes working together.

FAMILY CONNECTIONS

Genes obviously have quite a strong influence on who we are. We inherit them from our parents, one half from our mother and the other half from our father. But how many genes are passed on from our grandparents? And how many genes do we share with our siblings, uncles, and aunts? Find out here!

**Identical twins
100% shared genes**

**Siblings or fraternal twins
About 50% shared genes**

Aunt
About 25% shared genes

Parents—children
About 50% shared genes

Uncle
About 25% shared genes

Cousins
About 12.5% shared genes

Grandparents—grandchildren
About 25% shared genes

Half-siblings (same father or same mother)
About 25% shared genes

Adoptive parents and adoptive siblings
0% shared genes

THE BLUEPRINT FOR A HUMAN BEING

In 1977, independent of each other, two researchers, Walter Gilbert and Fred Sanger, developed the first techniques for determining the sequence of the letters (bases) on DNA. Reading off the letters in this way is called **sequencing**. At first, it was only possible to read individual, short DNA segments. But eventually, scientists wondered what it would be like if we could read the full blueprint for a human being by understanding the entire sequence of letters on the DNA.

It was a very tempting idea, especially because the DNA had to contain all of the information on human beings—everything that makes us who we are. Our appearance, our behavior, our way of thinking, why we grow old, why we become ill ... could we really find all the answers in our DNA?

But reading three billion letters of genetic code was an ambitious goal! Over one thousand scientists from 40 countries worked together to carry out this task. The Human Genome Project (human genome = complete set of genetic instructions contained in human cells) was born, and the first sequencing work began in 1990. Initially, the project made slow progress. Researcher Craig Venter planned to accelerate the process with a new sequencing method and announced that he would sequence the human genome single-handedly. A race to see who would be first began—Craig Venter or the scientists of the Human Genome Project.

However, the race ended on a note of goodwill: on June 26 2000, in front of running cameras, they announced together that they had succeeded in (almost) fully sequencing human DNA. The data was published in 2001 and two years later, 13 years after it began, the sequencing project was completed.

Had they finally solved the mystery of what makes us who we are? The results were amazing but also a bit disappointing: we have only 20,000–25,000 genes, hardly more than a fly or a worm. But surely the human body is far more complex? And are our mental skills not far more advanced? How could all human genetic information be stored in such a small number of genes? Plus, scientists discovered that only around 1% of our total DNA consists of genes. What was the purpose of the rest, the part of our DNA which was not used for the production of proteins? Some scientists began to refer to it as 'junk DNA.' Was all the other information (that is, 99% of our DNA) simply junk data?

It quickly became clear that although sequencing had provided a vast amount of new information, things were a little more complicated than expected. While scientists could now read the individual letters, they still did not understand the meaning of the words and sentences these letters formed.

And so, the end of the Human Genome Project also marked the beginning of a new project with the name ENCODE. Their aim was to examine the function of the individual genes and their interaction.

A gene is a section on the DNA

Hey, you! We have roughly the same number of genes!

The researchers discovered that a large part of what they had been calling 'junk' was in fact responsible for producing RNA. You already know about messenger RNA and transfer RNA, but here there were new kinds of RNA. These control which genes produce proteins and which do not. So, it is not only the number of genes which decides how complex an organism is, but also which genes are active. Scientists also came across something else: strange little attachments on the DNA and on the ball-shaped histone proteins around which the DNA is wrapped. In some places there were more, in others fewer of them. Soon they began to understand what an important role these attachments play.

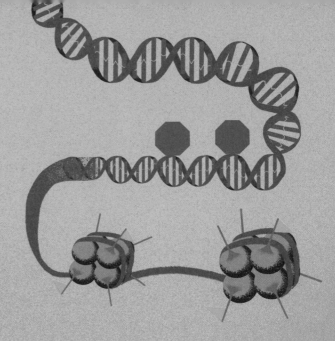

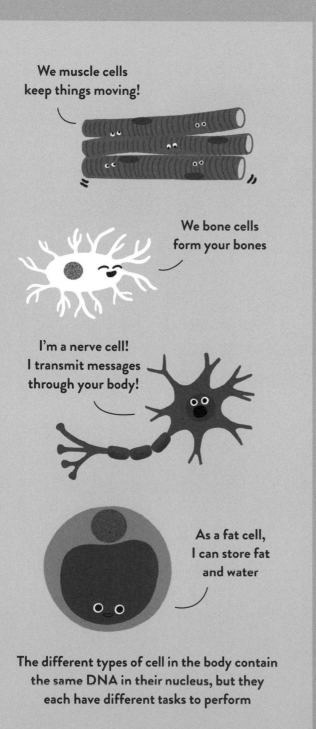

We muscle cells keep things moving!

We bone cells form your bones

I'm a nerve cell! I transmit messages through your body!

As a fat cell, I can store fat and water

The different types of cell in the body contain the same DNA in their nucleus, but they each have different tasks to perform

You may be wondering how it can be that the nucleus of every cell in our body contains the same DNA, but the cells can look very different and have very different tasks to perform? For example, how does a skin cell know that it is a skin cell and should only produce the proteins which are needed by the skin cell? This is where those attachments come in. They mark which genes are active and which remain inactive in the cells— or in other words, which genes must produce proteins and which don't. These markers remain when cells divide, so that the daughter cells will have the same attachments at the same points. This ensures that a skin cell stays a skin cell and that a skin cell can only produce skin cells. The attachments remind every cell in the body what its specific task is. They are the **cell memory**.

Researchers also discovered that the environment has a strong influence on where and in what quantity attachments are installed, and that they can be removed. This allows a cell to react very flexibly to changes in environmental conditions. Our diet, our experiences, whether we enjoy being at home or in school, whether we play sports or a musical instrument, or whether we have no hobbies at all. All these things influence us and leave traces behind—but for a long time, no-one knew how. Scientists were beginning to understand how environmental influences affect us and control our genes from the outside. At last, they had found the connection between the external world and our genes. They had discovered a whole new level of information and complexity. And because this information goes beyond the sequence of the letters of the genetic code, it is called **epigenetic** (from the Greek word *epi* meaning 'above').

To understand how important these epigenetic markers are, let's take a look at honeybees. Honeybees live together in large colonies. There is a queen bee who remains in the beehive, and her main job is to lay eggs so that new bees can hatch. There are also many, many worker bees that perform many different tasks, from defending the hive, to taking care of the eggs and larvae or collecting pollen and nectar. But they don't lay eggs. It's easy to distinguish the queen from a worker bee because the queen is much bigger, but how do these differences occur? Why does one egg eventually become a queen and another a worker? It can't be because of the letter code in the DNA of a queen and worker bee: that is identical. But if you look at the markers on the DNA, you can see that hundreds of a queen bee's genes have different markers from those of a worker. Why? While the queen bee is fed with 'royal jelly' throughout her development, the worker bees receive different food from a certain point on. It is the difference in their nutrition that determines whether a bee larva becomes a worker or a queen.

Queen and worker bees have the same letter code, but different markers.

Queen

Worker

The Human Genome Project was a global research project which aimed to sequence the entire human genome. It began in the year 1990 and was completed in 2003.

Epigenetic modifications are changes to the chromosomes which affect the activity of the gene, but not the letter code of the DNA. They are strongly influenced by the environment.

The goal of the ENCODE Project is to determine the function of the genes in the human genome. It began in the year 2003. DNA sequencing determines the sequence of letters (base sequence) on the DNA.

A genome is the sum of the genetic information of an organism.

MAKING COMPARISONS

Before long, scientists had also decoded the blueprints of other organisms, and researchers began to compare the genetic blueprints of different living beings. Some segments were identical in all organisms, and scientists believed that these segments were responsible for the essential functions of all organisms.

Scientists could also select specific differences and examine their effects. For example, if a certain segment is completely different in human beings to the segment in another organism, this section might be responsible for a trait which only occurs in human beings.

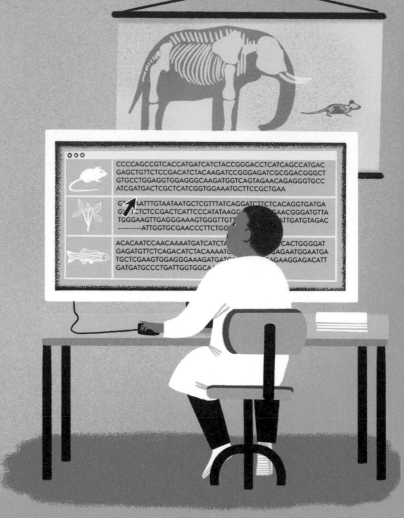

Scientists were especially interested in comparing human beings and chimpanzees as they are so closely related. Approximately 99% of the DNA of chimpanzees is identical to a human's. They vary by only about 1%. With three billion letters, that means around 30 million differences.

How have we developed since the evolutionary paths of chimpanzee and human separated several million years ago? We began walking upright, we lost (almost all) our fur, and above all, our brains have become much larger. The genes responsible for this had to lie somewhere in those 30 million different letters. One gene of interest for the development of speech had already been located: FOXP2, or 'the language gene.' This gene differs in different locations between chimpanzees and humans. Researchers believe that the changes to this gene played an important role in the development of human speech.

It's also possible to compare the DNA of different people. 99.9% of our DNA is identical, meaning only 0.1% is different (around three million letters). The reasons why we differ in our appearance, behavior, personality, and the likelihood that we will suffer from specific illnesses must be anchored somewhere in those three million letters. Now scientists hope that by examining the differences, they can learn which segments on the DNA are responsible for which traits.

In 2008, the 1,000 Genomes Project was launched to research the genetic differences between individuals and establish what effects the differences in the DNA have on the traits of individual people. The project reached its target of 1,000 genomes just four years later, and initial results were published. But the project continued to expand. This project is valuable because, by learning where our differences lie, we can begin to understand which differences lead to some people developing diseases while others do not. This helps us understand the emergence of diseases and allows us to develop medicines to treat them.

With a greater understanding of the genetic differences between us, we may begin to understand whether a medicine will be effective for a specific person and who will tolerate a medicine well. This would ensure that every patient gets the ideal medicine and avoids wasting time treating someone with a medicine which won't work for them. We could even develop therapies tailored to each individual person. This is what we call personalized medicine.

THE EARLY DAYS OF GENETIC ENGINEERING, OR HOW WE CHANGE THE BLUEPRINTS

You've learned how genes and the genetic code were discovered, and how scientists learned to read the code. Now it is time to look at how they began to *change* the genetic code.

To do this, we need to travel back in time again, to the year 1970! Scientists had just cracked the genetic code and learned how the blueprint was written. They did not understand everything yet, but at least they knew the letters and how words and sentences are formed.

Before long, researchers were already asking themselves the next big question, namely what would happen if the 'sentences,' the sets of information on the DNA, were rearranged. Changing the blueprints would be a momentous step that, once taken, would not be easily reversed. But their curiosity was strong, and in the end, curiosity won.

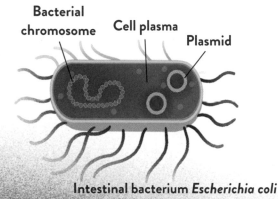

Bacterial chromosome   **Cell plasma**   **Plasmid**

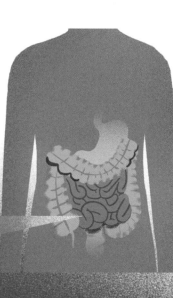

Intestinal bacterium *Escherichia coli*

Scientists found the tools they needed in bacteria. Bacteria are tiny, microscopic organisms, usually made of just one single cell. And bacteria are everywhere—in the air, in the soil, even inside you. Some can cause illness, but many are harmless and some are very important, like the intestinal bacteria which help your body digest food.

Researchers had been studying these bacteria for some time and had already discovered several interesting things about them.

Plasmids: little DNA rings found in the cells of bacteria in addition to the normal chromosomes. They are shorter and less complex than the normal chromosomes, which makes them perfect for making changes to DNA.

Cutter proteins: these work like scissors and can cut through the DNA at precisely defined points.

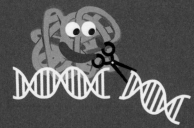

Binding proteins: they stick DNA segments back together like glue.

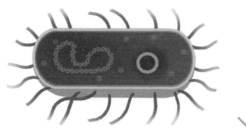

The very first experiments with rearranging DNA began in 1970, and in 1972, scientists combined DNA from two bacteria for the first time.

This is how they did it:

1

First, they fished the plasmids out of the bacteria.

2

Then they used a cutter protein to cut the two plasmids open.

3

A DNA segment from one plasmid was inserted into the other plasmid and the cut surfaces sealed again with the binding protein. The result was **recombinant** (rearranged) **DNA**.

4

This recombinant DNA was then reinserted into a bacterial cell. And hey presto! They had smuggled in a foreign gene!

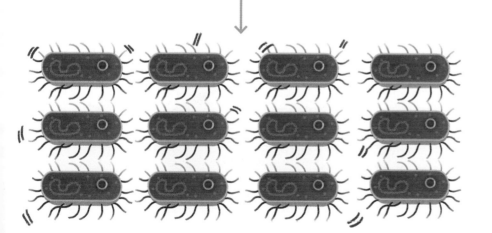

5

When the bacteria reproduced, the plasmids with the inserted foreign gene were now also reproduced. The bacteria became little factories producing the foreign gene in large quantities.

This was the birth of genetic engineering!

47

REMARKABLE MEDICINES

Scientists were now able to recombine and change genes as they wished. And because the DNA code is the same for all living organisms, it was possible to exchange genes between different organisms. Human genes could be smuggled into bacteria and reproduce, and if these genes contained the information to produce a specific protein, that protein was also produced when the bacteria multiplied. Later, scientists could extract the protein from the bacteria and use it to produce medicines.

The first medicine produced in this way was the protein insulin (licensed in 1982). Insulin is important because it enables cells to extract and process sugar from food. People who suffer from diabetes don't have enough insulin and frequently need to be given insulin from an external source. Previously, that insulin had been laboriously derived from pigs and cows. Now it could be produced very easily in bacteria. This human insulin is more effective, better tolerated, and, with the help of the bacteria, can be produced much faster and in greater quantities.

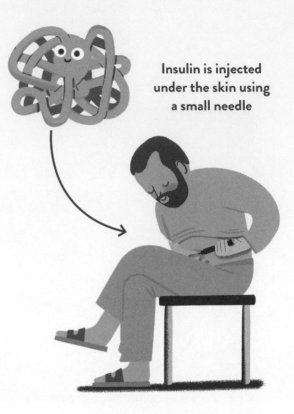

Insulin is injected under the skin using a small needle

The bacteria become insulin factories!

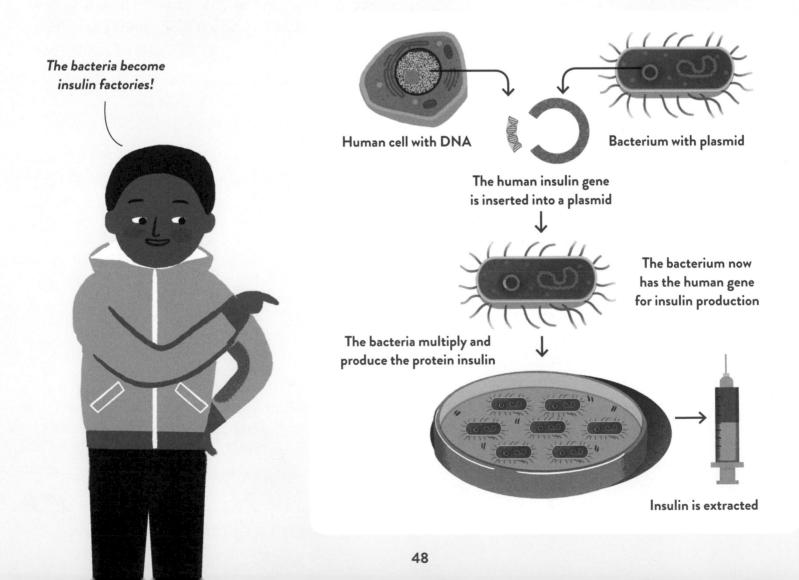

Human cell with DNA

Bacterium with plasmid

The human insulin gene is inserted into a plasmid

The bacterium now has the human gene for insulin production

The bacteria multiply and produce the protein insulin

Insulin is extracted

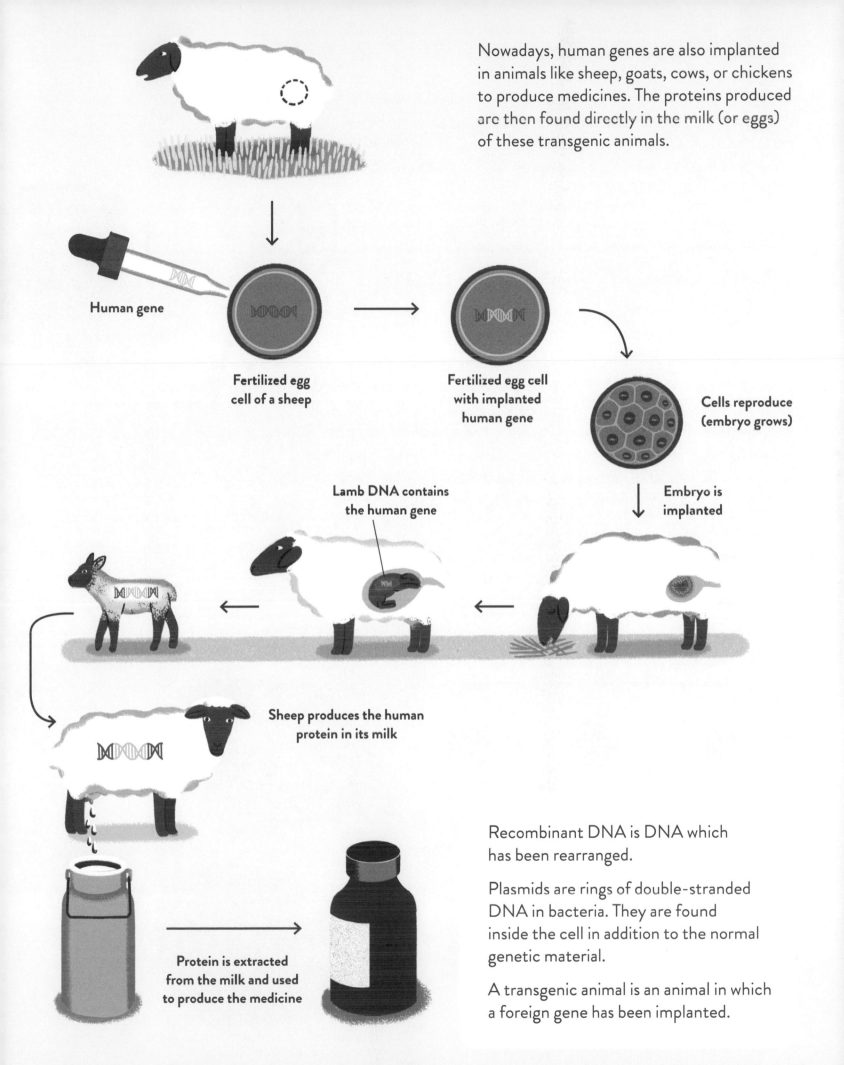

Nowadays, human genes are also implanted in animals like sheep, goats, cows, or chickens to produce medicines. The proteins produced are then found directly in the milk (or eggs) of these transgenic animals.

Human gene

Fertilized egg cell of a sheep

Fertilized egg cell with implanted human gene

Cells reproduce (embryo grows)

Lamb DNA contains the human gene

Embryo is implanted

Sheep produces the human protein in its milk

Protein is extracted from the milk and used to produce the medicine

Recombinant DNA is DNA which has been rearranged.

Plasmids are rings of double-stranded DNA in bacteria. They are found inside the cell in addition to the normal genetic material.

A transgenic animal is an animal in which a foreign gene has been implanted.

REPAIRING DNA

The more researchers learned about human illnesses and their causes, the more they wished there was some way they could intervene here, too. They already knew the precise location of a DNA error which resulted in a hereditary disease, so wouldn't it be possible to simply 'repair' the DNA?

This brings us to the subject of **gene therapy**: replacing the function of a faulty gene by inserting a perfect gene into the DNA.

First, the fault-free gene must be smuggled into the cells, usually through viruses. Viruses? Well, there is one virus you must have heard a lot about: the coronavirus. But there are many others. They are really tiny, even smaller than bacteria. They consist of genetic information (RNA or DNA) and an envelope into which this genetic information is packed. To reproduce, viruses penetrate the cells of the body and let the cells do the work for them. Soon, the cells are producing virus proteins and more viruses.

For gene therapies, researchers use the viruses as a sort of 'gene taxi.' They remove the genes which cause disease from the virus and replace them with the gene they wish to insert into the cell. When the viruses then penetrate the cells, they take the desirable gene with them.

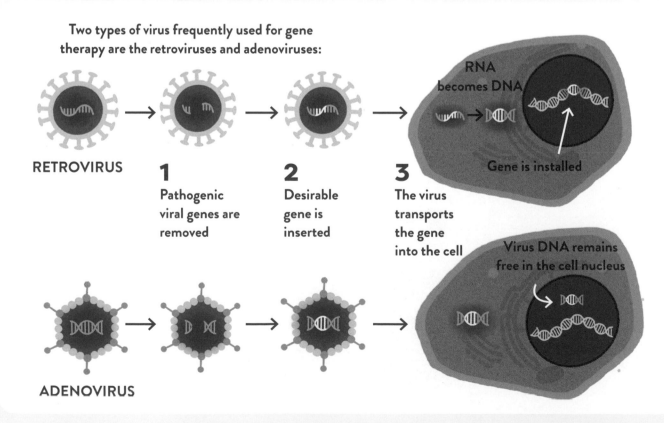

Two types of virus frequently used for gene therapy are the retroviruses and adenoviruses:

RNA becomes DNA

Gene is installed

RETROVIRUS

1 Pathogenic viral genes are removed

2 Desirable gene is inserted

3 The virus transports the gene into the cell

Virus DNA remains free in the cell nucleus

ADENOVIRUS

The very first gene therapy was performed in 1990, on a four-year-old girl with a very rare hereditary disease. Due to a defect in the ADA gene, her immune system was so weakened that the smallest infection, such as a cold, was life-threatening. For the gene therapy, doctors took a blood sample and transferred the fault-free ADA gene to her white blood cells with the help of a virus. These modified blood cells were then reinjected into her body. The treatment was successful. Many further studies have been carried out since then. There have been some major successes, and the first gene therapies have already been approved. But scientists still encounter setbacks. Why?

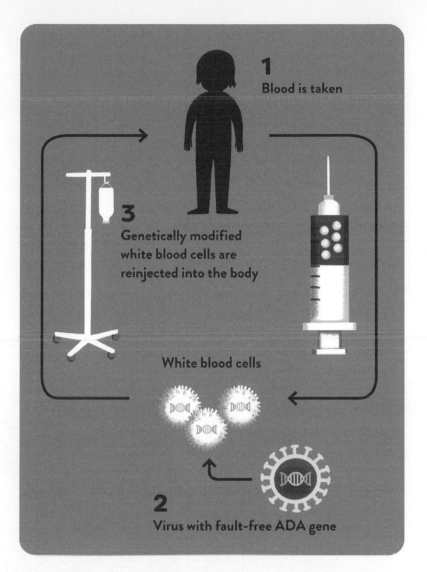

1
Blood is taken

3
Genetically modified white blood cells are reinjected into the body

White blood cells

2
Virus with fault-free ADA gene

One basic problem lies in the 'gene taxis'—the viruses. In the case of retroviruses, which insert themselves directly into the DNA of the body cells, the implanted gene remains and the treatment is effective over a long period. But there are also dangers here. It is not possible to control where exactly in the gene the DNA is added. The location is random. This means that the DNA could end up somewhere where it has no effect at all, or it might be added right in the middle of an important gene and destroy it, or it could suddenly activate a gene which causes cancer. Whereas the adenoviruses, which do not insert themselves into the DNA of the body cells, have the disadvantage that they are lost in the course of time and are therefore not effective for very long. Sometimes the body's immune system sees the viruses as a threat and fights and destroys them, so that the gene therapy has no effect. And if this battle against the virus is fierce, it can make the patient very ill.

In gene therapy, a healthy gene is implanted in the cells to take over the function of a defective gene.

CRISPR: THE GENE EDITING TOOL

Then came the discovery of CRISPR/Cas9, also known as CRISPR for short! This is a new procedure which revolutionized genetic engineering. But what exactly is CRISPR?

Scientists first discovered the so-called 'gene scissors' in bacteria, which use them to defend themselves against invading viruses. The gene scissors comprises of two parts. First, a 'seeker' searches for specific DNA sequences of enemy viruses. If the seeker finds this code sequence, it attaches itself at that point in the DNA to mark the site. Then the second part of the weapon, a 'cutter,' can precisely cut out the foreign genetic material.

Look out, here comes my DNA!

No way, José!

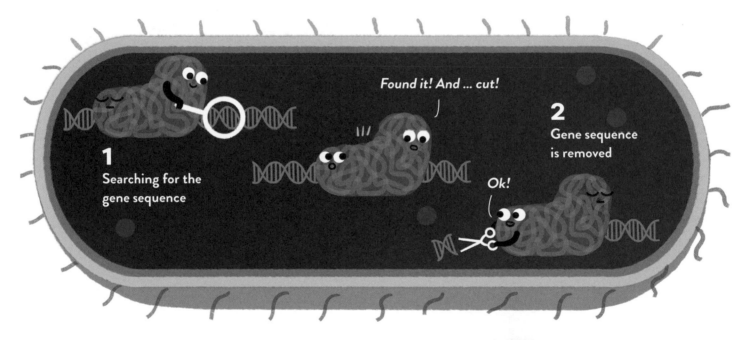

1 Searching for the gene sequence

Found it! And ... cut!

2 Gene sequence is removed

Ok!

Scientists Emmanuelle Charpentier and Jennifer Doudna were fascinated by this unusual weapon in bacteria and had the revolutionary idea of putting it to work for other purposes: as a tool for editing DNA!

The seeker could be programmed to detect any code sequence they wanted and steer the cutter to any site to remove specific genetic material. Repairs could also be influenced by replacing individual letters, removing sections of the gene, or adding completely new material. DNA could be edited! And though CRISPR has its faults, this method is simpler and more precise than any previous genetic engineering technique.

The seeker is programmed to locate a specific sequence of letters

This specific sequence of letters is located (in the DNA of the cell) and removed

The use of CRISPR in medicine has already been successful. At the end of 2020, CRISPR gene therapy was used against sickle cell disease (see page 33). Scientists have high hopes for this new technology, and many other projects are already in the pipeline.

But, like all great discoveries, this technology has raised some concerns. In 2018, Chinese media reported the birth of twins after targeted deactivation of a gene using the CRISPR technique. Previously, gene therapy had always been used to change body cells and was only effective on the person treated with the gene therapy. However, if the gametes are modified, these changes will also be passed on to following generations.

In other words, human beings had begun to make design changes to their own genetic blueprint. The world was in shock! Many researchers demanded that there should be an immediate global ban on experiments with human gametes and embryos, and we should define the rules for using this new technology. Obviously, it holds great potential for the world of medicine. Defective genes could be repaired before birth and many incurable hereditary diseases prevented ... but even if we do have that technology one day, is it right for human beings to interfere in the process of evolution? What are the possible consequences?

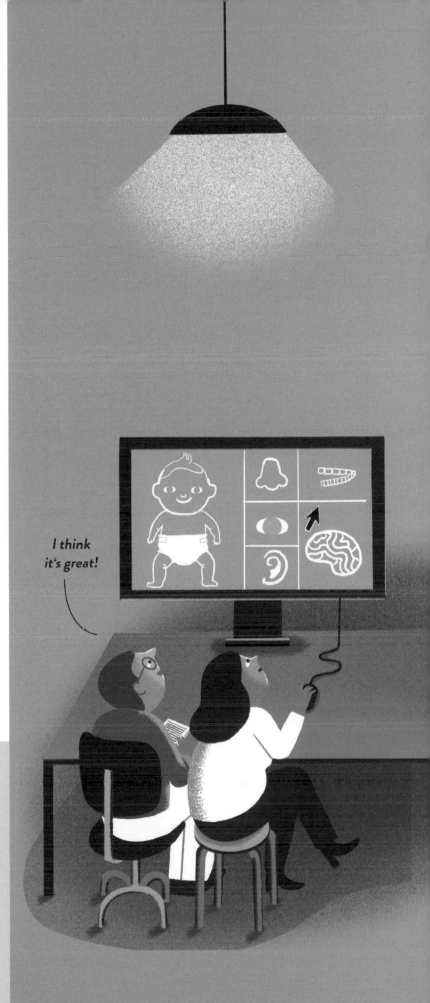

I think it's great!

CRISPR/Cas9 (for short: CRISPR) is used to change DNA in a targeted manner. The technique is also referred to as 'gene scissors.'

With CRISPR gene therapy, the gene scissors can cut out and repair a specific defect in the DNA.

A gene therapy in the body cells only affects the person who is being treated. A gene therapy which changes the gametes also has effects on the offspring of this person.

GREEN GENETIC ENGINEERING

Up to this point, people had cultivated plants based on the principle of selection. Changes in traits occurred randomly through mutations, and gardeners selected the plants with the most promising traits, crossed them, and repeated this over many generations. But this process was extremely slow! With genetic engineering and now with the CRISPR gene scissors, researchers hope that they will no longer need to wait for a desirable genetic modification to happen naturally. They plan to edit the DNA of the plants to make them resistant against diseases or specific insects and better adapted to specific environmental conditions, ensuring stable crops and better harvests. This would improve the food situation, especially in less economically developed countries. Scientists also hope to reduce the use of insecticides and other poisonous substances in this way.

They also believe it will enable them to fight vitamin A deficiency, which is a serious problem in less developed regions, causing hundreds of thousands of children to go blind every year. In these areas, scientists are breeding plants which contain higher amounts of vitamin A, such as 'golden rice.'

However, though this is a good cause, many people still take a very critical view of 'green genetic engineering.' Why? They are afraid that genetically modified plants could upset the balance of nature if artificially engineered genes are transmitted to wild plants; the risks for the environment are hard to predict; and some scientists also fear that we know too little about the effects on our health if we eat genetically modified foods. Also, green genetic engineering makes farmers financially dependent, especially in less developed countries, as they must pay a fee every year to use the new, improved seed.

Experts also argue about whether genetically engineered crops would really bring a reduction in the use of insecticides.

The use of genetic engineering in agriculture is known as 'green genetic engineering.'

SAVING THE ENVIRONMENT

We have just heard about the possible risks for the environment, but is it also possible that genetic engineering could help protect the environment?

You've probably heard of methane gas: one of the greenhouse gases and a major cause of global warming. A substantial proportion of this gas is produced by cows. Well, strictly speaking, it's not the cows themselves which produce the gas, but the bacteria living in their stomach. The gas escapes when cows break wind and burp. To reduce the quantity of methane gas in the atmosphere, we need to reduce the number of cows and eat less meat. Scientists are also working on changing the bacteria in the stomachs of the cows or the genetic material of the cows themselves so that the bacteria no longer produce methane gas (or only very small amounts of it).

Methane gas

Bacteria produce methane gas

Genetically engineered bacteria

Hey, I hardly ever burp!

Carbon dioxide is another example of a greenhouse gas. In 2019, a team working with researcher Ron Milo at the Weizmann Institute in Israel announced the development of a bacterium which, instead of sugar, feeds on carbon dioxide which it converts into sugar. They plan to engineer it so that it converts the carbon dioxide into fuels.

Researchers are working on the creation of bacteria which eat plastic

And there are other projects: bacteria which are genetically engineered to eat plastic, produce bioplastics, or locate toxic substances in the soil or water and eliminate them directly. Will these new technologies offer solutions for the problems which arose in the first place through the mechanization of our world? Or will they bring with them new problems which become increasingly unsolvable? Only time will tell!

GENE DRIVE

A **gene drive** sounds like something you might find under the bonnet of a car. In fact, it really does work like a turbocharger. A gene drive helps to spread changes to genetic material throughout a population at high speed. And it is used, for example, in the fight against malaria. If you remember, malaria is caused by parasites called plasmodia which are transmitted by mosquitoes. One way to prevent the spread of malaria would be to change the mosquitoes so that the plasmodia can no longer survive in them. In other words, to make the mosquitoes resistant to plasmodia so that they no longer spread the disease. But how can you make an entire population resistant? Let's just think how a resistance gene is spread within a mosquito population.

Resistance gene

Egg cell

Aha! The egg cell becomes the mosquito with the resistance gene.

Mosquito with resistance gene

If the resistant mosquito mates with a 'normal' mosquito (without the resistance gene), one half of their offspring will have a copy of the resistance gene, while the other half will not:

The ratio is 1 to 1.

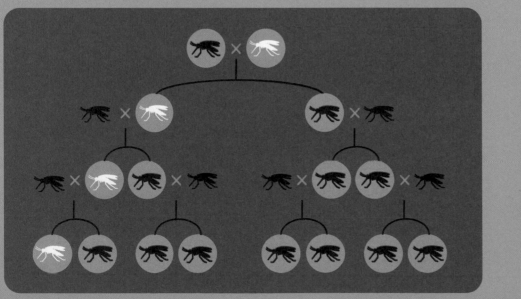

The mosquitoes with the resistance gene will pass this gene on to half their offspring. The illustration on the left shows what happens in the following generations. The resistance gene becomes rarer and rarer. In other words, spreading this gene is no easy job!

How can a gene drive help? The trick with this technique is to insert CRISPR gene scissors together with the resistance gene and program them to seek and cut out the 'normal' copy of the gene. The cell inserts the resistance gene in its place. And hey presto! The cell has two copies of the edited gene. And because the mosquito now has two copies of the resistance gene, it passes the resistance on to all its offspring.

And that's not all: the gene scissors become active again. They recognize the copy of the 'normal' gene after mating, cut it out, and replace it with the resistance gene. This means that all offspring now also have two copies of the resistance gene and pass it on to all their offspring, making them resistant.

And so on and so forth until, before long, all mosquitoes are resistant to plasmodia.

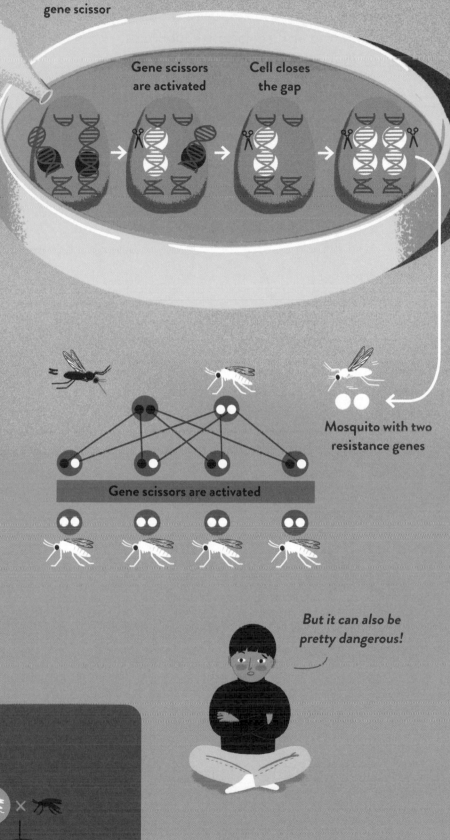

Resistance gene with gene scissor

Gene scissors are activated

Cell closes the gap

Gene scissors are activated

Mosquito with two resistance genes

Wow! That's quick!

But it can also be pretty dangerous!

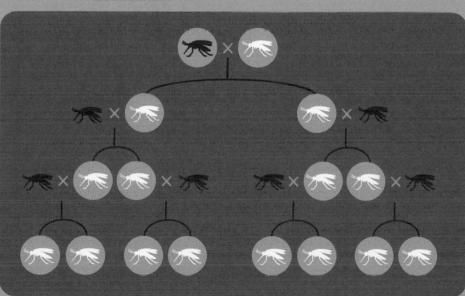

Brilliant—but also quite dangerous. After all, a whole population is being changed here. Once set in motion, it's virtually impossible to stop the gene drive. And what if unexpected side-effects occur? What would the consequences be? Just imagine!

DOLLY THE SHEEP AND OTHER CLONES

On February 22 1997, pictures of Dolly the sheep from Scotland hit the media all over the world. Dolly was unlike any other sheep because Dolly was the first sheep to be cloned from a body cell. Normally, for a lamb to be born, you need a male

gamete from the father sheep, the ram, and a female gamete from the mother sheep, the ewe. But for Dolly, scientists removed the nucleus from an egg cell and replaced it with the nucleus of a cell from the udder of a different sheep. The DNA was now the DNA from the udder cell. This meant that Dolly had the same genetic information in her cells as the sheep from which the udder cell originally came. Genetically, Dolly was identical to this sheep. A genetic copy is called a **clone**.

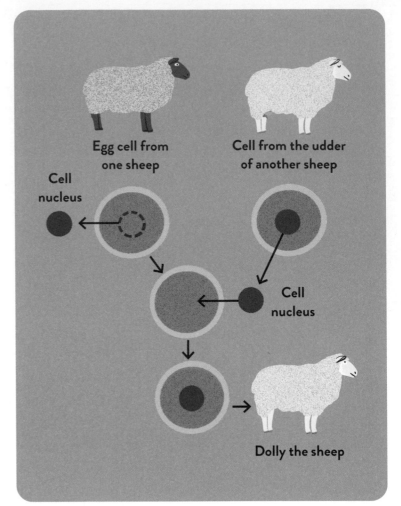

Egg cell from one sheep

Cell from the udder of another sheep

Cell nucleus

Cell nucleus

Dolly the sheep

Natural clones

Cloning is not unknown in nature. Some bacteria and yeasts reproduce by dividing into two identical cells. Many plants, such as strawberries, reproduce by means of offshoots which are clones of the parent plant. Identical twins are also natural clones. And when farmers graft fruit trees, they are cloning them. If a farmer has a fruit tree which bears particularly delicious fruit, he will take a shoot from this tree and attach it to the trunk of another tree. Then, when the shoot grows into a new tree, that tree will have the traits of the tree from which the shoot was originally taken. And the fruit it bears will be just as delicious, because what the gardener has done is to create a genetic copy of his favorite tree. A clone!

The idea of cloning animals wasn't new, either. During an experiment in 1962, over 30 years before Dolly, British scientist John Gurdon had already cloned frogs from random body cells.

But Dolly the sheep was the first cloned mammal. Scientists went on to clone cows, goats, horses, dogs, and other animals. And then, in 2018, Chinese researchers announced that they had cloned monkeys called crab-eating macaques. Dolly's birth in 1997 had already attracted attention, but these experiments on the macaques triggered a lively debate about cloning. Firstly, the process itself was problematical—almost 300 attempts were necessary to produce Dolly. Many lambs died before they could be born. Dolly was not healthy, either, nor she did not live very long. Above all, people were afraid that these experiments brought scientists one step closer to cloning humans. And, most agreed, that should be prohibited.

Just imagine that a copy of you existed, or a whole army of clones all identical to you. Or even that everyone on Earth looked the same, millions or even billions of copies of identical humans. A bit creepy, don't you think?

A clone is a genetic copy of an organism.

TINY ALL-ROUNDERS

Life begins with **embryonic stem cells**. They can develop into all sorts of cells, but this ability is lost after just a few days. The cells then specialize, becoming skin cells, nerve cells, blood cells, or one of the many other cell types. These specialized cells remain true to this one cell type. For example, skin cells cannot become nerve cells. It's a pity we don't have the embryonic stem cells later in life. If we did, we could create new, healthy cells from these all-rounder stem cells whenever body cells break down or no longer function properly. That would be fantastic!

In 2006, scientist Shinya Yamanaka conducted an extraordinary experiment. He succeeded in transforming cells from the skin into what are called **induced pluripotent stem cells** (or **iPS cells** for short). The name of these cells might be a mouthful, but it's certainly worth remembering, because we will be hearing a lot about them in the future. Like the embryonic stem cells with which life begins, these iPS cells can be transformed into all kinds of cells. But these cells can be produced from a fully developed body cell at any time. Scientists plan to use these iPS cells to replace damaged heart cells after a heart attack, for example, or to breed new, healthy nerve cells for people who are paralyzed. Scientists have great hopes that these cells will enable us to treat many illnesses which have been incurable up to now.

Embryonic stem cells can develop into all kinds of cell. But they are only found during the first few days of life.

iPS cells are generated from body cells which are returned to an early embryonic stage. They can be developed into cells of many different types.

Researchers hope that, one day, it will be possible to replace sick cells in the body and therefore treat many illnesses which are incurable at present.

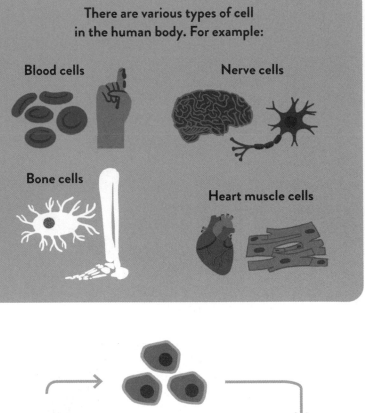

There are various types of cell in the human body. For example:

Blood cells

Nerve cells

Bone cells

Heart muscle cells

A skin sample is taken

Cells are reprogrammed to iPS cells

iPS cells are reproduced

Gene therapy

Cells are converted to the desired cell type

DINOSAURS AND OTHER PREHISTORIC GIANTS

I'm all for it!

Every cell in the body contains the full set of genetic information for the organism. And a complete organism can grow from a single cell. A frog, a sheep, a dog, a cat ... So, if we had the DNA of a long-extinct animal, couldn't we bring this animal back to life in the present-day world? Could *Jurassic Park* become reality after all?

The idea is not as far-fetched as it might sound! Scientist George Church from Harvard University in Boston is already working on bringing mammoths back to life. Although mammoths became extinct several thousand years ago, several well-preserved specimens have been found preserved in ice. Some were found complete with hair containing mammoth DNA. It had become fragmented over the course of time, but scientists have succeeded in almost completely decoding the mammoth's genetic blueprint. Church plans to insert mammoth genes into elephant DNA using the CRISPR gene scissors. This means that mammoths, or mammoth-like elephants, could very well walk the Earth again one day.

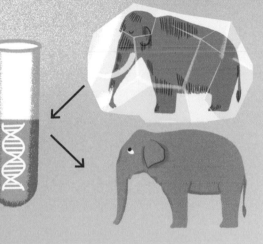

What about dinosaurs? Well, the problem with dinosaurs is that they have been extinct for many millions of years now, and scientists today do not believe it is possible for DNA to survive for such a long period of time, at least not in a condition good enough for them to use it. So *Jurassic Park* will probably remain science fiction!

CRIMINALS BEWARE!

Nowadays, genetic science even plays a major role in solving crimes. The tiniest traces of skin, hair, or blood found at the scene of a crime can help track down the criminal because these traces contain cells with DNA. Because the DNA of every individual is unique, it can be used to identify that person. The first crime was solved using a **genetic fingerprint** in 1987. But what is a genetic fingerprint?

Scientist Alec Jeffrey was studying hereditary diseases at the University of Leicester in England. He compared the DNA of different members of a family and was particularly interested in segments of the DNA where he found that sequences of letters in the genetic code were repeated, for example, 'CAGTCAGTCAGTCAGTCAGT.' These segments mainly occurred between the genes and were found scattered throughout the DNA. But what was their purpose? Jeffrey noticed that these sequences of letters were repeated different numbers of times in the DNA of different people. In one person's DNA, for example, there were five repetitions, in the DNA of another person 10, in that of a third person 20, 50, or 100.

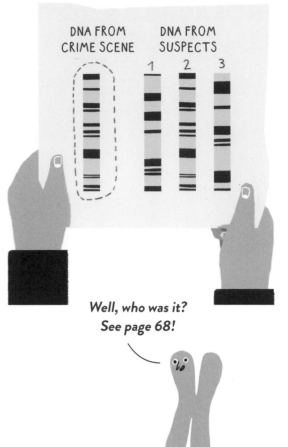

DNA FROM CRIME SCENE   DNA FROM SUSPECTS   1   2   3

Well, who was it?
See page 68!

Jeffrey realized that it was possible to identify a person based on the number of these repeated segments in their DNA. Not using just one location, of course, but with a combination of several such locations. He had discovered the genetic fingerprint! Before long, he was able to put the first criminal behind bars using this new method.

In its original form, the method was very complicated. But this changed as soon as they combined this method with a new technology called **PCR**, the **polymerase chain reaction**. PCR allows scientists to reproduce the tiniest traces of DNA millions of times! For detectives, this meant that only very small quantities of DNA from the perpetrator were necessary to produce a genetic fingerprint.

Can scientists now identify anyone with 100% certainty? Not quite! The DNA of identical twins is the same or at least very similar, so detectives must still rely on the classic fingerprint!

The genetic fingerprint is a means of identifying people based on the length of specific sequences of letters in their DNA.

The polymerase chain reaction (PCR) is a technique with which scientists can reproduce DNA, allowing them to identify even minute traces of DNA.

NEW VACCINES

At the end of 2019, the first cases of an illness caused by a new virus, Sars CoV 2, were reported. Soon, the virus was spreading around the globe and a race against time began to develop vaccines which could protect people against it. Completely new, genetics-based techniques were applied. Why? The basic principle behind 'traditional' vaccines is to introduce a weakened or inactivated form of the pathogen causing the illness (such as a virus) or simply individual proteins of a virus into the body to allow the immune system to get to know the pathogen and learn how to defend itself against later attack by the 'real' pathogen.

But this method is complicated and takes a long time. Genetics-based techniques allow doctors to react much more quickly. The decisive difference is that the new techniques no longer introduce the pathogen or individual proteins of the pathogen into the cells, but only the genetic information.

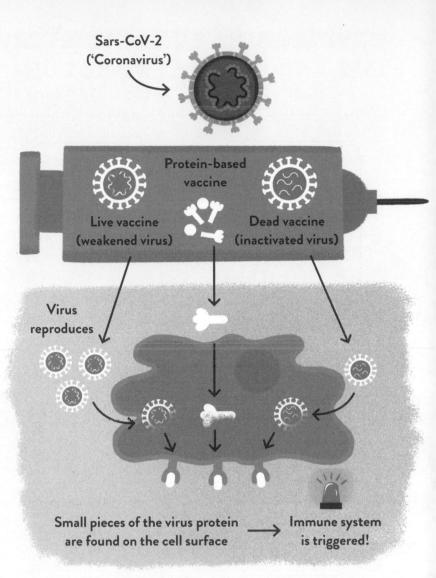

Sars-CoV-2 ('Coronavirus')

Protein-based vaccine

Live vaccine (weakened virus)

Dead vaccine (inactivated virus)

Virus reproduces

Small pieces of the virus protein are found on the cell surface → Immune system is triggered!

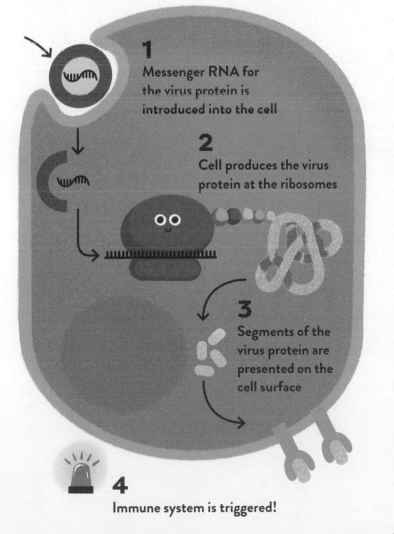

1 Messenger RNA for the virus protein is introduced into the cell

2 Cell produces the virus protein at the ribosomes

3 Segments of the virus protein are presented on the cell surface

4 Immune system is triggered!

The **mRNA** vaccines proved particularly effective in the fight against Sars-CoV-2. In these vaccines, the information on the foreign protein is provided in the form of messenger RNA (mRNA). In order to smuggle the messenger RNA into the cell, it is placed in an envelope of fatty substances which fuses with the membrane of the body cell, and the messenger RNA enters the cell. The cell now produces the foreign protein using the messenger RNA.

These vaccines then work like traditional vaccines: the immune system learns to recognize the pathogen, develops weapons against it, and mobilizes these weapons immediately against an attack by the 'real' pathogen.

Once scientists have found a suitable envelope, they can introduce any piece of genetic information from the pathogen into the cells. This means new vaccines can be developed and adapted quickly!

HAVE WE SOLVED THE MYSTERY OF LIFE AND OF WHAT MAKES US HUMAN?

We have traced life back to its origins. We have learned the language and cracked the code of DNA. We have read the blueprint of human life and found out a lot about ourselves in the process. Where we come from and what makes us who we are, our similarities and our differences.

And more.

We have discovered ways to change the blueprint artificially. We have dared to dream, putting our knowledge to use in the fight against hunger, climate change, and disease. And we have begun to make these dreams reality, but doubts remain. What if these new technologies have a negative impact? What if they trigger developments we did not expect?

And where do we set the limits?

There are still so many questions. Questions to which we have no answers. Secrets still to be revealed. Puzzles that you may solve one day.

YOUR OWN RESEARCH

Albino hedgehogs

In addition to the normal, brown-colored hedgehogs, white hedgehogs are sometimes also seen in the wild: albino hedgehogs. They lack the pigment melanin. As a result, they are white with red eyes. Albinism is a recessive trait. Think about it and draw a diagram of what will happen if an albino hedgehog mates with a normal, brown-colored hedgehog: could their direct offspring include albino hedgehogs?

Handy hint: albinism is inherited according to the same principle as the white blossom color in pea plants.

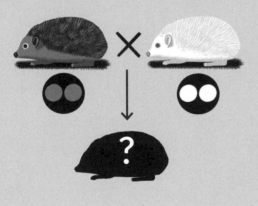

Your family tree

Try to trace how genes are passed on within your family! Find out who in your family can roll their tongue or has earlobes attached directly to the side of their head. Perhaps there are other unusual traits in your family: a dimple on the chin, red hair, blue eyes, freckles, etc. Collect information on as many family members as possible and put together your family tree. Draw each member of your family or stick photographs of them on a large sheet of paper, and write the information you have collected beneath each picture. Can you see patterns? If you have traits which are dominant, like dimples, one of your parents will also have them. However, many traits are caused by several genes together, meaning it can be difficult to predict how they will be passed on.

Karyogram

Study the karyogram below: according to the chromosomes, is this person male or female? And can you see anything else that is unusual?

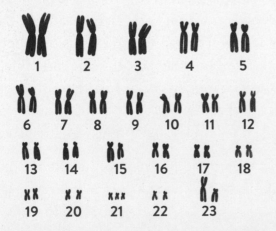

Cloning

Try cloning for yourself! Using a houseplant or a plant from the garden, cut off a fresh shoot about ten centimeters long, cut off any large leaves, and place the shoot in water. The first roots should form after a few days. When there are enough roots, you can plant your clone in a small flowerpot.

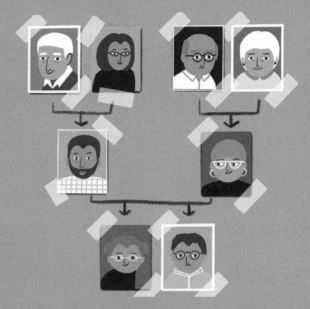

Answers on page 68

INDEX

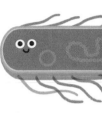

ANSWERS

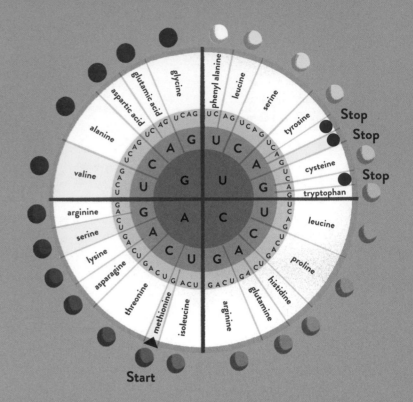

Karyogram

This karyogram shows an X and a Y chromosome. This means that the chromosomal gender (sex) of this person is male. In addition, it can be seen that there are three copies of chromosome 21 instead of only two. This genetic disorder is known as Trisomy 21 or Down Syndrome. You can find out more about Down Syndrome on the internet.

Page 30

Well, did you crack the code? Here's the solution: The sequence GUC stands for the amino acid valine. The sequence AGC stands for the amino acid serine. The sequence AUG stands for the amino acid methionine. AUG is also referred to as the start codon, because AUG defines the starting point for the translation, the point where the production of a new amino acid chain begins. The sequence UAG does not stand for an amino acid but is a so-called stop codon. It defines the end point of the translation, the point where the amino acid chain ends.

Page 62

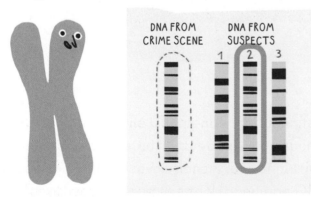

It was suspect number 2! This person's DNA barcode (pattern of lines) matches the DNA found at the crime scene. But how are these patterns formed? Certain DNA segments are duplicated, split lengthwise, and stained with dye. And as the length of the DNA segments varies from one person to another, different patterns are created. In this way, a person can be identified based on their unique DNA barcode.

Page 66

There will be no albino hedgehogs in the next generation, as the 'fault-free' copy of the gene (dominant) will override the faulty copy of the gene (recessive).

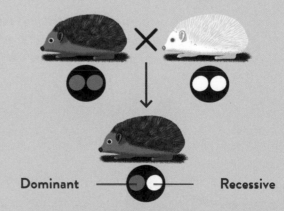

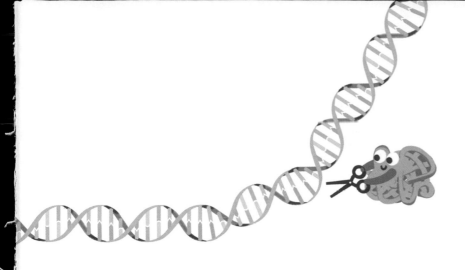

ACKNOWLEDGEMENTS

Carla Häfner:

My special thanks go to my family for their patience and understanding while I was writing this book.

I am also indebted to Dr. Jochen Graw, Heiner Götz, Dr. Ina Peters, Prof. Oliver Betz, and Dr. Wiebke Sauter for their useful suggestions and comments on my manuscript. In addition, I would like to express my heartfelt thanks to the many young test readers who made sure I never lost sight of my target group.

Mieke Scheier:

Thanks a million to my sister Marika, Tanja, Mone, Yuxing, Tomke, Mirko, Jens, Eva, Julian, and the rest of the team from the Rosenallee for countless looks, ideas, corrections, and the shared lunches.

Also, many thanks to my mother, to Fridolin and to Nola for their understanding, support, and encouragement!